FLYFISHING
for COARSE FISH

Pike • Rudd • Carp • Roach • Perch • Barbel
Chub • Zander • Dace • Tench • Bream • and other fish

This book is dedicated to two great men
taken from us too early.
Firstly, Hiram Garton, or 'H' as most of us knew him;
a true gentleman as well as a passionate angler.
Also to James Holgate,
a key man in my growth as a writer.
Both are sadly missed; never forgotten.

FLYFISHING
for COARSE FISH

*Pike • Rudd • Carp • Roach • Perch
Barbel • Chub • Zander • Dace
Tench • Bream • and other fish*

Dominic Garnett

Merlin Unwin Books

First published in Great Britain by Merlin Unwin Books Ltd, 2012
ISBN 978-1-906122-38-6

Text and photographs © Dominic Garnett
   (see also Acknowledgements page 11)

Published by:

Merlin Unwin Books Ltd
Palmers House
7 Corve Street, Ludlow
Shropshire SY8 1DB, U.K.

The author asserts his moral right to be identified as the author of this work.
British Library Cataloguing-in-Publication Data:
A catalogue record for this book is available from the British Library.

Designed and typeset in Bembo by Merlin Unwin.
Printed by Star Standard International Ltd.

Also published by Merlin Unwin Books
www.merlinunwin.co.uk

The Secret Carp Chris Yates £17.99 Hb
Falling In Again Chris Yates £17.99 Hb
Confessions of a Carp Fisher BB £20 Hb
Pocket Guide to Matching the Hatch Peter Lapsley & Cyril Bennett £7.99 wiro
Pocket Guide to Fishing Knots Peter Owen £5.99 Pb
The Fisherman's Bedside Book BB £18.95 Hb
Beginner's Guide to Flytying Chris Mann £9.99 Hb
Fishing with Harry Tony Baws £15.99 Hb
Trout in Dirty Places Theo Pike £20 Hb
Complete Illustrated Directory of Salmon Flies Chris Mann £20 Pb

CONTENTS

FOREWORD
by Bob James

My own adventures with coarse fish on game tackle began in the pages of *Mr Crabtree Goes Fishing*, where I read with great excitement about casting a fly for quicksilver dace and greedy, lumbering chub. Some of my fondest memories of the time were on the River Wey, watching flies hatching and casting for these very fishes. The challenge was often to identify which of the two species was rising - the dace needed a split second flick of the wrist, but with the big-mouthed chub my quirkier solution was to say 'God Save the Queen' before striking, which rarely failed.

This book is a practical guide to this exciting branch of fishing. It's true to say that flyfishing for coarse fish is no modern fad, but until now no one has produced an up to date guide. I can think of nobody more keen or articulate than Dominic to take up the challenge. In spite of his younger years, I've found him a real kindred spirit and very much a writer with his heart and soul in the right place. He is always highly readable, but what I like most is the spirit of his work. Like Bernard Venables or Chris Yates, the aim is no ego trip but to capture the joy of fishing and take you to the waterside, rod in hand.

Times may have changed since Mr Crabtree, but all sorts of fish still take a fly with gusto. After all, what did you think they were eating before we turned up with boilies and pellets? The list of species you can catch is a long one, many of which you'll find in these pages. Quite why so many of us confine our flyfishing efforts to trout and salmon is something of a mystery to me, but perhaps says more about fashions in the sport than any true order of merit. As crazy as it sounds, once upon a time salmon were seen as a nuisance on southern rivers such as the Avon, and in fact pike were often a far more highly prized catch. Coarse fish can be every bit as challenging and rewarding as 'game' species.

Looking back over the years, perhaps the biggest change in fly fishing has been the vast improvement in tackle. I rarely get sentimental about fishing gear, especially when I remember the kit we once used. Early nylon fly lines were grisly, whilst the silk versions had to be carefully dried out after (and often during!) every fishing trip. For today's angler, quality tackle is widely available. On this score, you'll find Dominic's advice on using today's gear clear and easy going - he is totally conscious of tackle and tactics, but not obsessed.

Along with advanced tackle however, today's fishing landscape seems dominated by a 'size is king' approach, just as in previous generations the match scene led to a preoccupation with competition. Maybe it is time to redress the balance and get back to fishing for the sheer joy of it.

Flyfishing is certainly hugely enjoyable, but I don't wish to give the impression that it is purely an amusing diversion. It is quite often the best way to catch. For example, I remember one fly fisher creating quite a stir by making match winning catches of coarse fish on the Nene. Look elsewhere and you'll find specimen fish of many species, from giant pike to large chub, tempted on fly tackle. But whatever the catch, big or small, flyfishing for coarse fish is a wonderfully absorbing challenge.

A guide like this is long overdue and so it gives me great pleasure to introduce not only an intriguing new fishing book, but a fresh and engaging voice in this exciting branch of the sport. It may be Dominic's first book, but I'm pretty sure it won't be his last.

INTRODUCTION

Anglers are strange creatures at times. Just like the local tackle shops, we draw up neat, easily-distinguished fishing categories: coarse, sea and game. But while such labels remain, a growing number of us are less easy to classify, seeking new methods and experiences. And why indeed not? The fish themselves couldn't care less which box we fit into.

A lot of the most interesting fishing comes when different methods blur and a healthy cross-fertilisation of ideas occurs: and tackling coarse fish with a fly rod is an especially fresh and exciting area. There are few fish that cannot be taken on a suitable fly with a little thought, and many of our best-loved species respond excellently to this elegant method. Indeed, it could change your entire approach to fishing.

But why cast a fly for coarse fish in the first place? Why not just use bait? The short answer is: for simple pleasure and excitement. From the sight of a big chub sucking in a hopper to the wild rush of a pike grabbing a fly right by your feet, you won't find a more intimate or visually thrilling way to fish.

My own belief is that in today's world of artificial baits, bite alarms and self-hooking rigs we are putting more and more barriers between ourselves and the fish we want to catch. Flyfishing puts us back in direct contact. We are aiming to immerse ourselves in their environment and understand their habits better. Our best assets in this field are not expensive tackle or fancy baits but our eyes, our feet and our brains.

The pursuit of flyfishing should not be regarded as elitist. It should be for everyone to enjoy and with just about any species in mind. It is not 'superior' to bait or lure fishing - practises which are also artful and enjoyable. Our ancestors have a lot to answer for with their snobbery that deemed certain species as unworthy - a stupidity that still has an echo in angling today. And yet we find that luminaries of the past from Falkus and Buller to Richard Walker were all well aware of the thrill and effectiveness of flyfishing for coarse fish.

Perhaps the only barriers are thus the clichés some still adhere to. Above all, I wish to demonstrate to the coarse anglers that flyfishing needn't be a fanciful, fussy or technical affair. In reality it is refreshingly simple. It's certainly no rarefied art form or self-imposed handicap. On the

contrary, on its day it can be the most effective method of all.

Equally though, I want to show game anglers that the so-called 'coarse' species can be every bit as fun and challenging as trout and salmon. They are also a great deal cheaper and less exclusive: for the amount it costs to catch a handful of stocked trout many coarse fishing clubs offer a season ticket.

My stance in writing this book is to provide a series of useful footholds for anyone who wishes to pursue the art of flyfishing for coarse fish. Those with existing knowledge of flyfishing may need to bear with me through some basics which others will be grateful for, although fly casters may also learn a trick or two from coarse angling tackle and techniques. It is not an exhaustive guide – and nor should it be. Too much of angling has been dissected and subjected to ready-made solutions. In flyfishing for coarse fish the field is wide open and I hope this guide will be the start of your own discoveries, ideas and a deep enjoyment.

Perhaps it is time for a quiet revolution in the fishing world. Perhaps it is time we went back in search of fun rather than figures. Perhaps it is time for angling to become a little less impersonal, a little more dapper; less techy and a little more intimate. The next time someone asks what type of angler I am, I'm simply going to shrug my shoulders.

ACKNOWLEDGEMENTS

I am grateful to my brother Alex Garnett for the diagrams on pages 61, 79 and 128. Additional photography, with the author's thanks, has been kindly supplied by the following:

Ian Nadin: back cover and pp 21, 122, 138
Simon Steer: 14, 16, 19, 26, 28, 41, 53, 54, 60
Frazer McBain: 104, 105, 109, 110, 136, 137, 141, 155, 203
Paul Hamilton: 29, 40, 98
James Callison: 12, 108, 117, 118
Sam Edmunds: 64, 85
Bob James: 96, 97, 174, 176, 178, 180, 183
Steve Lockett: 27, 102, 131
Seb Nowosiad: 51, 128, 130, 169
Jo Bliss: 52, 115
Rob 'Norbert' Darby: 70
Jim Smith: 46
Russell Hilton: 74, 125
Dave Smith: 10
Furzebay Carp Lakes: 112

The author would also like to thank:
Steve Partner at *Angling Times*, for all your support.
Bob James for his invaluable expertise on barbel and other tricky areas.
Nigel Savage, for his invaluable input on zander fishing and predator flies.
Gavin Burn, Lucy Bowden and all at Hardy Greys. Steve Lockett – for film work and press.
Merlin, Karen and all at Merlin Unwin Books for all your kindness and assistance with the book.
John Garnett, for introducing me to fishing as a boy, even after I fell in the Thames and you had to fish me out.
Jo Bliss, for putting up with my fishing and other quirks.
Tom Legge, for your encouragement.
Steve Cullen at *Total Flyfisher*, for all your honest feedback and encouragement.
John Horsfall – for friendship and fly tying tips.
Rob 'Jonah' Darby, Ian Nadin and Seb Nowosiad (the 'Piking Pole' who somehow made it onto the cover because, in his own words, 'I'm so bloody handsome.').
My mother for a thousand and one reasons.

And a big shout to: Jim Smith, Dicky Fisk, Theo Pike, Paul Hamilton, Steve Moore, Andy Lush, Leon Guthrie, Zyg Gregorek, Nick Maye, Chris Gooding, Pete Thomas, Juha Vainio, Ron P. Swegman, Toby Russell, Ben Garnett, Russell Hilton, Chris Lambert, Dave Smith. Steve Ormrod and all at the PAC. Andy Parkinson and the motley crew at Exeter Angling Centre.

For continuing fishing exploits, articles, photography and custom flies visit the author's site: www.dgfishing.co.uk
Coming soon: *Fly Fishing for Coarse Fish – The DVD*, a film by Steve Lockett (Three Wise Anglers Productions) featuring adventures in search of roach, rudd, carp and pike.

A large, soft-meshed landing net is a must for coarse species. A padded mat is also a good idea to protect your catch, which will often be lifted onto the bank since wading is not always an option.

TACKLE

Before any discussion of the fish we want to catch, some basic principles on tackle and technique are essential. I make no assumptions about prior knowledge – everyone has to start somewhere and the tackle and terminology of the flyfisher will be new to many coarse anglers. On the other hand, game fishers may also want to take a few notes from the coarse angling side – some of the tackle and ideas could prove most useful.

In essence flyfishing should be a simple, stealthy approach. With little more than a rod, reel, flies and a few other sundries you are free to roam. Since it is a 'stalking' method, this mobility is a great asset.

Fly Rods

Fly rods are very simply rated with two numbers: the length of the rod (usually in feet and inches) and the line rating (a number from 1 to 12 followed by # or AFTM). For example, a Greys GRXi 9' 6" 6/7wt, indicates a 9½ foot rod suited to casting 6 or 7 weight lines. The lower the line rating is, the more light and flexible the rod will be and the finer the fly line it will cast.

The range of rods on offer is phenomenal. Let's take a couple of simple examples: A short, 7 or 8ft rod with a line rating of between 2 and 4 would be a delicate little tool, perfect for dace or small chub on an overgrown river where space is tight. At the other end of the scale, a 10ft, 10/11wt rod would be a suitable tool for casting giant flies on a windy lake for pike. Sadly there is no one model suitable for everything. Rather than provide a confusing array of options here however, each species of fish has its own neat summary of recommended tackle in the relevant chapter.

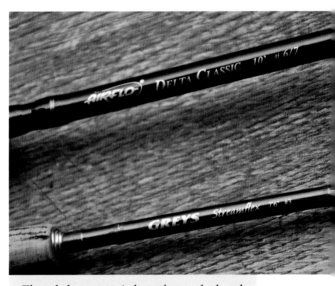

Fly rods have two vital numbers – the length and the recommended weight of line. Here we have a long mid-weight all-rounder (top) and a little wand for tight spaces and light lines (bottom).

It's also worth mentioning that you should always choose carefully and buy the best rod you can afford. Fly rods tend to cost a little more than coarse rods – but high quality gear has come down in price and you needn't spend a fortune to get a useable casting tool.

ONE SIZE FITS ALL?

With the huge range of waters and species involved, there is no single set-up that will adequately cater for all your needs where coarse fish are concerned. Hence the likelihood of the 'what do you need another rod for?' debate! Joking aside, if you were pressed into taking just two set-ups, a good choice would be an 8ft 4wt for sneaking to the river or in pursuit of silver fish, whilst a dependable 9ft 8wt will handle both carp and a spot of light pike fishing.

Reels

Whilst a well-made fly reel is a beautiful object, an expensive model is quite unnecessary for those starting out as it is less important than a quality rod and fly line. Nevertheless, look for a light model of suitable size. Reels have line ratings just like rods – and it can help to actually fasten a reel to the rod you will use to check it's a good match before parting with your money. A decent drag is also important, especially for those fishing for bigger species. The drag is usually a small adjustable wheel, which should be set to give out line when a fish runs hard.

The reel is perhaps the least important part of your set up – but it still pays to buy the best you can afford. Look for something that balances your rod well and has a reliable drag.

A light, well-balanced small stream outfit. This set up, designed for 3wt lines, would be great fun for dace, roach and small chub at close quarters.

Fly Lines

Fly lines come in many types and sizes but we can classify them fairly simply into floating, intermediate and sinking lines. Always match the line number (sometimes given with the letters AFTM or #) to your rod: the higher the number, the thicker and more powerful the fly line will be.

Nine times out of ten, a floating line is the fly angler's first choice, since the floater is the easiest to cast and use. These are brightly coloured so you can pick them out easily – the fish don't seem to mind even quite loud colours, provided the line sits crisply on the surface. If you tackle only shallow water, say up to 8ft, you may only ever need a floating line.

An intermediate is a slow sinking line, used when we are targeting fish lying slightly deeper in the water. For greater depths and bottom-hugging fish we then have sinking lines – these often have a 'di' or depth in inches rating, for example a 'di-6' would sink at six inches per second.

Whichever the density, lines come in a few simple types:

Weight Forward (WF) is the most common, which simply means the fly line

Fly lines come in many types, but the simple floating weight-forward (WF) is the only one required for much for your fishing.

is tapered with a thicker first few yards for easy casting.

Double Taper (DT) lines have a tapered, thicker section at each end of the line, meaning that when one end becomes worn it is possible to simply take the line off and load it in reverse to give you a fresh start.

Shooting Heads (SH) are lines with an ultra-thick first few yards – these are primarily for distance casting.

Many anglers would be best advised to forget the jargon and simply invest in a quality Weight Forward floating line. Don't buy cheap for the sake of a small saving – a quality line will give you better performance and ease of use.

Sink Tips & Poly Leaders

It is also worth mentioning these briefly. They can be handy for both casting purposes and for making quick changes in presentation. 'Poly leaders' provide an intermediary length of line between fly line and leader. They can help make your casts 'turn over' smoothly, thus aiding presentation.

They are attached loop to loop style and come with different floating or sinking properties just like fly lines. The other bonus here is that quick adjustments can be made – for example, a quick sinking poly leader could be added to a floating line to get your fly down to deeper-lying fish without the need to change your whole set-up.

Leaders & Tippets

When a flyfisher talks about the 'leader' he means the length of thin, clear line attached to his fly line (ie. think of the 'leader' as going first). This is slightly confusing because the term 'line' usually refers to the coloured fly line itself and not the clear section we attach our flies to – the leader.

How long should your leader be? For obvious reasons, you may well want to avoid the thick end of the fly line landing too close to the fish because they may spook. Longer leaders also allow flies to sink deeper and behave more naturally. Ten to twelve feet is perhaps the ideal starting amount: but this could drop to as little as seven or eigth feet in a cramped space where trees are a problem. Equally, we might want to increase the length if the fish are easily spooked.

Hand-tied leaders are typically made of different sections of monofilament or fluorocarbon line – to give a typical example: three feet of 15lb strength mono at the 'butt' end next to the fly line, followed by lengths of 12lb, 8lb and finally 5lb line to make a leader that gradually goes from thick to fine. This is so that when we cast, everything 'turns over' properly and the leader straightens out smoothly from thick to thin rather than landing in a heap.

By far the simplest solution is to buy a readymade, shop bought 'tapered leader' however. These are available in various lengths and breaking strains, perform excellently and save both time and hassle.

You will also hear fly anglers talking about the 'tippet'. This is the final part of the leader and acts like a coarse angler's 'hook length' – it is a short, finer section of line onto which the fly is tied.

Leader and tippet materials are a matter of personal preference. Modern flourocarbons are tough and tangle-resistant but sink quite freely: hence their suitability for wet fly fishing. Mono is the obvious choice for dry fly, or slower-sinking presentations, and the new flexible 'copolymers' make very fine, supple tippets.

A final point for bigger fish or larger flies is that knotted, multi-section leaders are usually avoided in favour of a single length of line. When carp fishing for example, knots are kept to a minimum to avoid potential weak points and so we may use a simple ten-foot length of straight 8lb mono between the fly line and our fly.

Mucilin line floatant and fuller's earth: two essentials for the flyfisher which offer a quick fix with correct presentation.

SOME ESSENTIAL SUNDRIES

Fly Vest

With the fly angler's requirements for lots of small items of tackle, a fly vest is a must for many of us. It also keeps us mobile – rucksacks and other bags can hinder casting and are a nuisance when wading.

Polarising Glasses

Another absolute must. Firstly, these protect your eyes from wayward casts and flies travelling at speed. However, you will spot many more fish with a good pair than you could ever hope to see with the naked eye, as well as locating snags, weed and other interesting features.

Floatant and Sinkant

Always worth carrying in a pocket, mucilin can be applied to the end of the fly line to help it float crisply. A little smear can also be used to help your dry flies float, although other products such as 'gink' may be preferred.

It is also worth carrying a sinking agent of some kind – 'Leada sink' or Fullers Earth are two such options. These will help wet flies and leader materials sink when applied – which can be vital to get your tackle performing as desired.

Another critical use for such products is to 'degrease' your tippet, however: applying a little sinkant removes the shine from monofilament which can deter fish from taking.

Tungsten Putty

Found in the carp section of tackle shops, this heavy, mouldable substance is invaluable for quickly adding weight to flies or leaders. A classic example is on a river when your fly is riding too high in the water to reach the fish. Unlike split shot it doesn't damage the line either.

Tungsten Putty is useful stuff – a quick pinch added to fly or tippet is invaluable when you want to get down deeper to the fish. Unlike shot it won't kink the line.

Forceps

A pair of forceps is vital for unhooking fish. Some pairs will also de-barb hooks. A useful way to keep a pair to hand at all times is to attach them to a 'zinger' style pull-cord device on your fly vest. Use fine tipped forceps for smaller species – although a foot long pair will be required for pike and zander.

A pair of quality forceps is useful for debarbing flies as well as unhooking fish. This is highly recommended for smaller species.

Coarse anglers using bait always replace hooks between sessions to keep a sharp edge. With flies, which might see several outings, a hook sharpener is the answer.

Above: A landing net head doubles as a useful place to keep line out of bankside snags.

Below: For bigger fish, it's wise to step up your kit. A large net, mat and decent-sized forceps are sensible steps. I also like an accurate set of quality scales.

Hook Sharpener

One of the most overlooked but useful items in the angler's pocket, a hook sharpener is always a good investment. Unlike bait fishermen, fly anglers rarely change hooks and a well-used fly will inevitably lose its edge in time. The few seconds it takes to hone the edge of a hook could save you the frustration of missing a fish on the strike.

Nets

Unless you're fishing for tiny fish such as dace, a net is a must. Portable, collapsible nets are useful for those who wade but for the bank angler, a two piece landing net with a long handle is highly recom-

mended. Size depends upon species: carp and pike demand a big net. Larger is better. Go too small and you could risk damaging your catch or losing the fish of the season. Since coarse fish are to be released, a modern soft mesh net is advisable rather than stringy, old-fashioned trout models.

Unhooking Mat

An unhooking mat is a smart investment for the bank angler. This protects your catch, preventing damage on the bank side, and I would go so far as to say carp and pike anglers should not fish without one. If you want a picture of that special

Many coarse fisheries demand a large landing net and unhooking mat – good practise for safe catch and release, especially where bigger fish may make an appearance.

catch, a damp well-positioned mat also ensures that any dropped fish has a safe landing.

My mat has a carry handle and is spacious enough to accommodate a large, collapsible landing net – ideal for roving. A mat can also be used to cover brambles and other obstructions on the bank where your fly line may otherwise get stuck. It can also form a makeshift seat, protecting your backside as well as your catch!

Waders

Whilst not absolutely essential, it's surprising just how many anglers don't own waders. These can open up areas you'd never otherwise reach and are especially useful to the river angler. They can also take away the need to remove fish from the water for handling and unhooking purposes, thus preventing needless damage and stress.

Waders are available in various types and sizes. Thigh waders are fine for small, shallow streams but chest waders let you tackle deeper areas. Alternatively, a good compromise are 'waist waders' which are essentially wading trousers.

The cheapest and most straightforward option with waders is a pair of complete 'boot foot' waders. 'Stocking foot' waders require additional boots, and the cost quickly rises, although these tend to be higher quality and very comfortable.

Also pay attention to the grip on the soles of your wading boots. These come in either 'cleated' or 'felt' (or if in doubt, some soles come half and half). Cleated are just like the grips on wellies – ok for general use, but for slippery and rocky bottoms, felt soles are much more secure. You can also affix studs to any soles for extra grip – worth considering if you fish on rivers with strong currents and sections of flat, slippery rock.

A wading staff is also a good idea in testing waters, to provide extra stability.

Wading should always be done with caution. Stony-bottomed rivers can be pleasant to wade but silt and mud can

Often over-looked for coarse fishing, waders will take you to the parts of the lake or river that other anglers can't easily reach.

be treacherous stuff. There is also the question of whether you actually need to wade? See the tips section (*page 196*) for more on this subject.

Right: For some anglers, nothing beats the feel of traditional tackle. These beautiful cane rods belong to Juha Vainio, who uses them to tame bream and ide – besides trout – on Finnish rivers. The glass of gin and tonic is optional.

FLIES & FLYLIFE

'The world is full of magical things patiently waiting for our wits to grow sharper.'

– Bertrand Russell

It is a curious fact that many anglers have only a very limited idea about the natural diet of their quarry. Coarse fishers habitually introduce artificial baits into the water to encourage the fish to take the hook bait. Fly anglers seldom have this as an advantage. To develop as flyfishers we need to become more attuned to the life in our waters and this means as active investigators, always on the lookout for clues which may help.

Whichever type of fish we target, the fly angler's challenge is both simple and infinitely variable: to present an artificially-tied fly in a manner that convinces the fish that it is a living thing, or at least something worth eating. Our task requires imagination and is very different to the challenges facing the bait fisherman.

So what counts as a 'fly'? Anything and everything from a tiny black gnat to a 6in pike streamer could be called a 'fly'. The trout fisherman will find some familiar fly patterns in these pages but others that will be entirely new.

Of course, there are also 'flies' which imitate nothing at all in nature. For example, flies resembling maggots or even dog biscuits can be used to catch fish. Is this still flyfishing? Some traditionalists would say not. Personally I would prefer to imitate natural life of some kind. On the other hand, such 'flies' are still fun and effective to use. They could also be a good starting point for anglers switching codes from bait to fly or tackling those fisheries where the fish are well-accustomed to taking artificial baits. My aim is to avoid traditional snobbery and so I make no apology for including a few examples of 'bait' flies in these pages. For the most part however, our starting point here is the natural world.

As Nature Intended?

The good news for all anglers is that you won't need a science degree or a grounding in Latin terms to uncover the hidden world of the waters we fish, just a healthy curiosity and a willingness to look. A basic, working knowledge will indeed suffice. There are many dozens of caddis fly varieties for example – it could take years of study to become an expert. But all share common characteristics and with only a limited fly selection we can still catch plenty of fish. Coarse fish, especially, seldom worry if the fly is exactly right. If it is presented when the fish are feeding and makes an acceptable impression, it is likely to be taken. To draw a random parallel, there are many types of pizza. Some I like more than others but all are pretty edible if I'm hungry. Except the ones with prawns on them – they're just plain wrong.

It is also fair to say that some of the coarse fishes have an extremely wide-ranging diet. You're unlikely to go spooning the contents of a carp, and in the absence of solid evidence 'general fit' patterns can be used to bluff our way to bites. Specific knowledge is useful however and will add a depth of intrigue and satisfaction to your fishing.

REVEALING QUICK DIPS!

Five minutes with a dip net in the margins of the water is a fun way to find out what might be on the menu for the fish: in this case, in the margins of a small, weedy pond we found freshwater shrimp, hog lice, corixa (water boatmen) and even baby newts.

Those already versed in trout flies will find coarse fish a fresh challenge, taking the angler to new places and catering for different feeding habits.

Don't feel that understanding natural bugs and flies comes only from books. Wherever you fish, a little investigation can be carried out. In a river, for example, just turning over a few stones will tell you which nymphs and invertebrates are present. A pond dipping net could reveal a great deal in the margins of a lake – or simply taking a quick study in the margins of the water for evidence of hatching or drowning insects. The fish themselves are the most obvious clue of all. Are they making splashy rises, or sipping gently? What are they rooting around for on the bottom? Wherever you decide to fish, a good deal of flyfishing is about simply looking carefully.

Important Flies & Prey Items for Coarse Fish & Anglers

So what are the most important natural prey items for coarse fish? While there is no short answer, a handful of key groups are pretty much universal. Specifics (ie size, colour, quantity) will vary from water to water, but a useful rough guide is presented here along with sample artificial fly patterns in each case. Do also note that while there is overlap, coarse fish exhibit their own unique tendencies. Even the same species' feeding habits vary between different habitats and times of year.

Bloodworms & Buzzers (Chironomidae)

Bloodworms are a staple diet for many coarse fish and often the most plentiful natural food source, particularly on lakes and ponds. Even the muddiest, most featureless little pool can be rich with these little creatures which are actually the larval stage of a group of insects that fly anglers call 'buzzers' – meaning all kinds of smallish dark insects such as midges. Crucially, these also hatch year round, even through the winter.

The bloodworm itself is small and segmented, usually less than 1cm long, living amongst mud and debris. They are

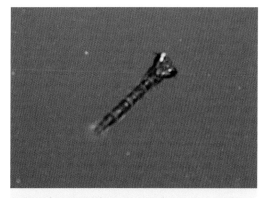

A midge pupa, known as a buzzer to anglers.

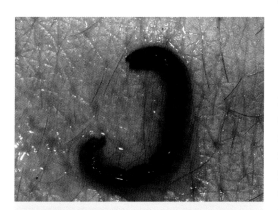

The bloodworm, Chironimid (midge) larva.

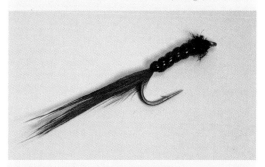

The bloodworm immitation fly.

often red, hence the name 'blood' worm, but can also be brown, olive or other colours too. Fish such as bream, carp and tench love to grub around for these and often betray their presence with trails of bubbles or by puffing up clouds of silt.

Bloodworms are very difficult to imitate in this dormant state, but are of more interest when they begin their ascent to the surface to hatch into adult insects. Starting from the bottom, they slowly rise through the water layers. They are especially vulnerable in this state and mid-to-surface feeders such as roach and rudd especially will actively pick them off at this stage, which is imitated with flies simply called 'buzzers'. Again colours and sizes can vary from tiny, pale larvae to large dark samples. Flyfishers often try to copy these slowly-rising nymphs with suitable copies.

At the surface each buzzer must then hatch out and escape from the water if it is to live on and breed. Fluffy 'breathers' protrude from the insect and poke through the surface before the insect sheds its skin or 'shuck' and makes good its escape. Many are not so lucky and coarse fish, just like trout, will often gobble up buzzers when they are emerging at the surface and highly vulnerable. Hence an 'emerger' fly is a good option here, which sits just at the surface to imitate a buzzer in the process of hatching.

The final stage is the adult buzzer. These are represented by flies such as the classic Black Gnat, and are sometimes energetically attacked by fish as they return to the water to lay eggs.

Freshwater Shrimp (Gammarus pulex)

Another almost universal aquatic creature, the fresh water shrimp forms a vital part of the diet of many fish, from small to large species, offering a protein-rich staple. Distinguished by their seven pairs of legs and sand hopper-like appearance, they vary from grey to yellowish brown in colour and can be found on most streams and rivers but also thrive on weedy still-waters.

Coarse fish will happily browse weedy or rocky areas for these creatures, which themselves eat mostly plant and waste matter. Several suitable imita-tions exist for the fly angler, who will find an artificial fly especially useful on running water. Roach, chub and barbel are amongst many species which prey on shrimp.

A very similar species on still waters is the hog louse. These are generally a little bigger and scruffier looking – but can also be mimicked with similar fly patterns. A Buggy Hare's Ear or Grey Czech nymph

are both suitable flies for louse and shrimp feeders.

The freshwater shrimp, Gammarus pulex.

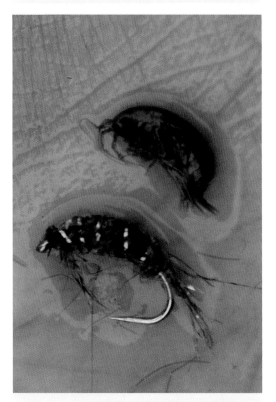

The freshwater shrimp alongside a suitable copy. The artificial shown here is little more than a ribbed Hare's Mask, with a few strands of partridge for legs.

Caddis larvae, showing variations of attire, and the best of camouflage.

Caddis or Sedge Flies (Trichoptera)

On almost every water in the land, from a wide river to a tiny canal, you'll find caddis flies. Just to confuse everyone, fly anglers often refer to these as 'sedge flies'. Frequently mistaken for small moths, they are distinguished by hairy double wings and two long antennae. Most are brown or dark and drab in colour, often 1cm or larger in size and are especially active in the evening. When you see splashy rises on the surface just before nightfall, sedges will often be the cause and fish such as chub can be just as partial to them as trout. They are certainly a species to excite the fish and on drains and canals I've watched egg-laying adults pursued by excited rudd that were virtually jumping out of the water to catch them.

The larvae and the adults are of interest to fish and anglers alike. Caddis nymphs are easily recognised by their little cases which many varieties make for themselves from small stones and debris.

The adult sedge, a big skittering fly.

Caseless caddis also exist but whether cased or otherwise, bottom-feeding fish such as bream and barbel like to grub around in search of these. The real fun starts as the fly struggles to the surface to hatch, however. These fairly large, fluttering creatures are especially vulnerable as they emerge and can herald some exciting fishing. Some types head for the safety of the bank in frantic fashion, making a v-shaped wake on the surface. Chub in particular can give spectacular takes when this happens, clobbering these unfortunates in no uncertain fashion.

Mayflies & Olives (Ephemeroptera)

When you hear anglers speak of the 'mayfly' they usually mean the large, cream-coloured river flies of summer. However, there are also a good many smaller mayflies which can be found throughout the summer months and even into autumn. Flyfishers confuse everyone by referring to the many smaller mayfly varieties as 'olives'. Blue winged olives, pale wateries and olive uprights are just three common examples. Both the nymphs (ie immature larval stage) and the adults are of interest to river anglers.

Coarse fish that thrive in faster water such as chub, dace and barbel all predate on these 'mayflies' and those who fish running water would be well-advised to do a little homework on their river; turning stones in the shallow, well-oxygenated areas will quickly indicate numbers and varieties of nymphs present, whilst adults can be studied as they hatch.

The olive upright dun (inset).

A pale watery nymph.

A carbon copy of the natural fly isn't usually required but a good general rule is to try to look for a rough match in terms of sizes and colour to mimic the naturals found. Mayflies are also present, albeit less predominantly, on lakes and still waters where species such as the pond olive may be present. I have even spotted the large, classic mayflies hatching on a rural canal.

WATERBORNE OR WATERDROWNED?

So-called terrestrials may often be peripheral or seasonal sub-plots to the trout angler – but not so with coarse fish. With species such as carp and chub they can form the mainstay of artificial patterns. Presentation varies between hatching insects and 'accidental' casualties for obvious reasons: the former rise from the lake or stream bed to emerge into the air, whilst the latter make the opposite journey! In such cases making a beetle or moth descend with a healthy plop, something you would never do with a mayfly, could be just the way to attract attention from a hungry fish.

Other differences are also stark – traditional dry flies are often well hackled to leave a 'footprint' on the water like a resting insect. Terrestrials, on the other hand, are often better presented as exposed, waterlogged victims, drowning in the surface film rather than sitting on it.

Terrestrials

The term 'terrestrials' simply refers to any flies or creepy crawlies that live on the land but accidentally end up in the water. Daddy longlegs are a classic example, blown onto water in high winds. Fish will often make the most of such 'free gifts', which can also provide a great opportunity for the angler. Flying ants are another good example – these poor fliers turn up in hundreds for short summer spells. Inevitably some end up waterlogged and various fish species take them with gusto.

A terrestrial beetle, trapped in the surface film.

A grasshopper.

Caterpillars fall into rivers from banks and overhanging trees, becoming easy prey to chub and other coarse fish.

Countless other species make up a varied menu that can be great fun to imitate for the creative angler: beetles, grasshoppers, caterpillars, moths… the list is endless.

Fingerlings, Fry & Bait Fish

From minnows and fry to a whole range of other prey fish, any anglers targeting predatory coarse species are advised to establish what the dominant 'fodder' fish are on the waters they fish. Bleak and minnows are common prey for river perch and zander for example, whilst larger roach, perch and bream are often the staple diet of pike.

Of all the coarse species, the predators are perhaps the least fussy about detailed, specific 'copies' of what they are eating. Movement and flash are often enough to provoke a feeding response. Even so, some detective work can be rewarding. In the autumn, for instance, massed concentrations of fry can be found

The motherless minnow (Leucaspius delineatus) – like fry, these provide rich pickings for perch and jack pike on countless drains and small waters.

on lake shores. A good tip is to offer something just a little bigger to stand out from the dominant mass of prey items.

Another point worth noting here is that at certain times of the year almost all coarse fish can turn predatory, even the usually docile bream and rudd. Tiny fry patterns can yield interesting results at the right time of year.

Snails

These are another overlooked but often vital food source. Carp and tench, especially, love them and will gorge on them in weedy areas of still waters. The best opportunity of all can arise in hot weather when water snails are found on the surface or clinging to weed growth in great numbers. Floating snail patterns can work, but for some reason the simple Peacock and Black fly is still arguably the best *(see page 205 for this fly dressing)*.

The freshwater snail.

The Black & Peacock Spider. Not a close representation of the natural, but a fly that seems to work excellently wherever fish are eating snails.

Tiny Treats

There are times when coarse fish, like trout, will pick off tiny creatures on the water's surface. Caenis or 'smuts' are the classic: tiny white or pale insects which are widespread on many waters. Aphids are another staple micro-food item on bushy streams and lakes. Fish like dace, rudd and roach are all partial to such delicate prey and it can really pay to have a few suitably titchy flies in your box, right down to size 20 and smaller.

Other Common Critters

The angler could literally spend a lifetime discovering the many fascinating living things in and around water – but we must finish our quick tour of coarse fish food with the remaining notables.

Damsel flies form several varieties and are hugely widespread. The pretty adult insects are only occasionally snatched by fish – but the nymphs are an important prey item throughout the milder months. Chub, perch and carp are just three fishes which will take them.

The corixa or 'water boatman' is another creature found everywhere and distinguished by a dark back, shiny underside and two kicking paddles. It is readily eaten by many fish species.

The corixa, or water boatman.

The artificial corixa.

SIZE DOES MATTER

One problem of switching the focus to coarse fish with fly tackle is that the vast majority of existing patterns are geared towards trout. Not only do coarse fish have highly varied preferences for food, they also have very different sized mouths. Hence you'll find quite a dramatic range of fly sizes and designs within these pages.

Static or Twitched Fly?

It is ultimately your choice how flies are presented.

A few points commonly recur however:

• Is the aim to emulate something natural, or stimulate a response?

• Does the target species feed delicately or aggressively?

Every rule has exceptions, but most coarse fish, except the out-and-out predators, prefer a fly presented with minimum interference, allowed to drift naturally with the speed of the river current for example, or indeed left completely static on the bottom. A good general rule is to use less agitation and go subtle for shyer, browsing fish (roach, rudd, carp etc), bolder for more predatory fish (chub, perch, pike).

Trigger Points and Hot Spots

Many trout flies feature so called 'trigger points' of colour and flash to entice the fish. A gold bead or contrasting tag of bright colour are two typical examples here. Coarse species can also respond to such stimuli, but are often much less aggressive than trout or salmon, hence 'drab' can work better. This does depend on species however: the flash of a large, gold-headed nymph could attract a hungry chub, for example, but a shy roach is likely to react with fear or suspicion.

Water quality is also a prime consideration. In muddier or coloured water an extra dash of colour can help the fish locate the fly; clear water in which the fish can study artificials more carefully often demands greater subtlety. Whichever way you prefer your fly patterns, a hint of contrast or colour is almost invariably better than overkill.

Above: Most natural nymphs and flies are drab in appearance. Hence in clear water, our artificials don't need to shout too loud.

Some of the flies taken by coarse fish are tiny and the corresponding artificials need to be suitably small – as these caenis demonstrate, along with an artificial spinner tied by Andrew Baird.

This pike was active and wanted a loud fly, in spite of the temperature being -6°C!

PIKE

If there is one species which truly shatters the cliché of flyfishing as a genteel sport, it is the pursuit of *Esox Lucius*, the pike. A creature of acute predatory instincts and a frightening turn of speed, pike are a quarry to fray the nerves and fire the imagination. Once seen as the scourge of many waters, today's anglers are finally discovering not only the role pike play in a balanced fishery but the sheer excitement they bring on a fly rod.

The good news for the predator angler is the wide variety of waters which hold pike: from canals, rivers and drains through to lochs and reservoirs, sport can often be had at good value and moreover, right through the colder months of the year when other species are not an option.

From wild exaggerations to outright lies, pike still suffer from something of an image problem in some circles. Mindless killers they are not: the pike is a toothy, temperamental beast and for those willing to take up the challenge, the species is as engrossing and fascinating as any you care to mention.

PIKE TACKLE & SEASON

TACKLE: A 9-weight rod is ideal for most pike fishing and my staple choice. 10-11 weight rods are useful for extra-large flies and big waters, whilst an 8 weight can be fun for small water piking where snags are few and mostly jacks are expected. A floating fly line may be all that is required for shallow waters of up to 8ft or so. For greater depths, intermediate and sinking lines may be necessary – or alternatively sinking poly leaders. Look for fly lines with a meaty, weight forward taper – several companies now produce special lines for predator flyfishing.

Leaders: 6-10ft of mono or fluorocarbon (minimum 15lb strength) connected to a 16in wire trace which is vital to prevent bite-offs (see trace notes). As a rough guide your leader and trace should be about a rod's length for floating lines, or 2-3 feet shorter with sinkers.

Other: A large landing net, extra long forceps and a padded unhooking mat are 'musts' for the safe release of this deceptively fragile predator.

SEASON: Oct-March is the traditional season and pike will feed even when temperatures plummet below freezing. Summer piking is also possible, but great care must be taken when oxygen levels are low and pike are vulnerable.

Whilst many species can be fished for with adapted trout gear, the pike is another matter altogether, demanding a very different approach and specialised tackle. Heavier rods and lines are necessary not only to cast the comparatively big pike flies, but to deal with powerful lunges and set hooks in tough, bony mouths. A less well-known fact about the pike is its fragility and I would urge any would-be pike angler to treat the fish with respect and forethought – knowledge is key here but a handling session with an experienced pike-fisher is also well advised.

Bitten

My own encounters with pike on a fly rod form some of the most vivid experiences of my fishing life. Such was the case some years back on a bitterly cold morning by a little canal. It had seemed a stupid day to fish, with freezing temperatures and icy

The shimmer of a flashy pattern tempted this pike form a dark Finnish lake.

winds – to be truthful I had gone out only because it was my last chance of some escape before a fresh term of teaching English to badly-behaved teens. Within minutes, my fingers were shivering as I searched the reeds with a gaudy orange fly. The hail soon arrived, but where were the pike?

Casting into a little gap on the far bank, the fly stopped dead in what I assumed to be a submerged branch or other obstacle. As I gave another tug to pull free, the line crept to life between my fingers. There was a great, sudden rush of power and in five seconds flat the 'snag' shot twenty yards down the canal, fly line pelting after it. I had caught plenty of pike by conventional means but this was another experience altogether! The monstrous fly suddenly didn't seem so very big in such a huge toothy mouth. I was converted.

Starting Points

Pike, wherever you find them, are lovers of two things important to their survival: prey fish and cover. The successful pike fly angler is a searcher, trying to establish where the fish are, where they feed and where they lie up. It is essentially a game of hide-and-seek in which we must use any clues available, or at worst apply some educated guesswork. Areas where prey species congregate, where you encounter weed and submerged snags, or sudden changes in depth are all a likely bet for pike, which are seldom evenly spread or accessible at our convenience.

As deadly-efficient predators, pike

*In pursuit: a jack pike follows a fly right
along the margins. A quick twitch provoked
an immediate reaction – but on this occasion
the assailant missed.*

behave differently to other species. They don't browse on small food items except during periods where the water is dense with fry. Rather, they seize larger prey whole, in short but dramatic feeding spells. The 'mood' of the fish is thus critical. If we can identify the 'when' as well as the 'where' the fish feed, so much the better. There is a sliding scale at play here – with blind hunger at one end and total apathy at the other. Whilst generalisation is dangerous, it seems that certain conditions tend to work in the pike angler's favour time and again: early and late in the day, for example, when pike use low light to sneak up on prey. Overcast conditions also tend to encourage pike activity more than bright spells – although on bigger, deeper waters, sunny days can also be excellent.

The water rocks as a decent fish nears the net. By all means enjoy the fight – but try to land pike safely and quickly. A short, sharp battle is better than exhausting the fish.

The detective work is down to the angler, which is perhaps what makes pike fishing so absorbing.

Flyfishing with Bite

Naturally, there are also other considerations for flyfishing. As flies appeal primarily to sight-hunting pike, water clarity is vital. Less than ideal water can be countered with big, bright flies and those with vigorous movement, but chocolate-coloured water is a waste of time. It's also worth pointing out here that water clarity

CASTING FOR THE CRAMPED

Where casting space is at a premium, a little improvisation is called for. The way to avoid obstacles is to utilise all available space – which might not be straight behind you. Steeple casts are useful where you might need to throw your line up and over steep banks and hedges to the rear. Another good option is to present the fly parallel to the near bank margin (pictured) with the use of side casts. Sometimes we're so keen to hit the far bank, we bypass those pike lying close in, often right by our feet.

can vary immensely even on the same fishery – on a windy lake for example, exposed shorelines may be churned up but a little further out the water may quickly clear (pike and other predators sometimes use these colour-change zones to attack from). Similarly, on canals or drains some areas may be far more clear and settled than others. The active, hunting angler can take the initiative and find the favourable water.

Flyfishing has inevitable similarities with lure fishing. One disadvantage is the lack of vibration of flies compared to vigorously-moving lures. However, flies can be fished effectively at far slower speeds and there are definitely times when pike are unwilling to chase a fast-moving target, requiring more time to make a grab. On such days, often in cold conditions when fish are sleepy, the fly can comfortably out fish lures.

There is a lesson here in retrieve speeds and the flyfisher should be willing to experiment. It is a mistake to think that flies need to be stripped at breakneck speed for them to be taken; and a lively, attractive retrieve needn't mean a rapid one. On days when pike are actively chasing prey, or in waters where the pike are not subject to much fishing pressure, a spirited, pacy presentation can be deadly. But at other times, a slower figure-of-eight retrieve with a few little tweaks thrown in will prove more effective. Remember, the fluidity of the fly means that even small movements on the fly line will convert into an attractive motion. To my mind the best retrieve is one that possesses a happy combination of allowing the pike enough time to react, and yet enough movement to trigger a bite.

There is undoubtedly a knack to a successful retrieve, but I would advise any pike flyfisher to try a small, clear water such as a quiet drain or canal for initial forays because a great deal can be learned by watching how pike react to a fly.

Smashes and Grabs

The subject of pike 'takes' is an area of fascination in its own right, but for all those full-blooded attacks where the fish tears off with the fly you will find just as many takes in which the fly is intercepted with a great deal less violence. The bigger fish especially can give surprisingly gentle indications.

Watch a pike mouthing a fly and the reason becomes clear. Far from grabbing the target in a wild flurry, all a fair-sized pike needs to do is open its jaws and the vacuum created makes even a large fly disappear with minimum effort. All you might feel on the fly line is a gentle knock. It pays to be vigilant and watch the fly line.

On other occasions, your only clue might be the fly line moving curiously to one side. Indeed, if the pike moves towards you as it takes hold, you may get only the barest indication that something is happening.

A canal crocodile! Good pike can turn up on any water – so you should always carry a decent-sized net and mat.

Some of the other bites pike deliver are utterly unmistakable, pulling the rod round and rendering grown men into gibbering idiots; but all the rest need striking. Because of the species' bony mouth, firm contact must be made to set the hook. I prefer to do this by pulling firmly on the line and bumping the rod back sideways to set the hook – an upwards strike can simply pull the fly out of those jaws. The tough mouth of the pike is another reason why strong line and a rod with backbone are essential. If the fish bite gently or you don't connect firmly enough, you may well feel the fish grabbing hold for a few seconds before your quarry simply lets go and the line falls slack.

Drains, Canals & Small Waters

Perhaps the biggest surprise to date in all the journalism on pike flyfishing is how little focus there has been on the cheapest and most accessible fishing for them of all – the countless miles of canals and drains from the little-used canals of England and Wales to wetlands such as the Fens and the Somerset Levels. Just about all contain pike and exciting possibilities for the adventurous angler. I would also include in this category slower, human-altered rivers.

These narrow waterways also form the perfect introduction to the sport. Distance casting is unnecessary to reach the fish and, with the water clarity often good, the fishing is intimate and visually thrilling. It's also possible to fish a little lighter and to ditch those formidable ten

HIT THE FAR BANK

A great tip for consistent accuracy on drains or canals is to start with a short line, slowly taking more line off the reel until you have just enough flyline to reach the far bank and no more. By doing this you will find the line will shoot the perfect distance every cast, stopping dead by the far bank. This technique also helps to turn over a big fly, straightening the leader and giving good presentation.

weight or greater set-ups and huge flies which can be so off-putting to the unini-tiated. A nine weight is ideal, or even an eight where snags aren't severe, coupled with sensible-sized pike flies in the 2-4in bracket. Indeed, such smallish flies quite happily 'match the hatch' on many waters where the staple prey item will be small roach and perch. Such waters are often rich places and although you are less likely to tangle with titanic pike, there are often plenty there to offer consistent sport on even the coldest days of the year.

On even the most prolific drain, however, the fish are seldom evenly spread and the only way to catch is to keep moving and searching, looking for signs at all times, be they snags or other features, baitfish concentrations or those areas where waterways broaden or alter. Intersections between drains are a particular favourite – just like on a busy road, the junction is often the spot where a sudden crash is likely to occur!

Other narrow waterways may be pretty featureless to the casual observer – until you take a closer look. Sections can vary greatly in depth or clarity – inflows will muddy the water for example, whilst sheltered or elevated stretches might be consistently clear. The other obvious factor is that of other water users. Some canals see regular boat traffic in certain areas, in which case an early start may be required to cash in before the water gets too disturbed.

One consistent feature of every man-made channel is the shelf or 'drop-off', where the shallow margins slope down into the deeper water of the middle. This is an absolutely key area for all predators, which love to use this slope as both an ideal ambush spot as well as a 'lane' via which they can move undetected. I remember learning the importance of drop-offs some years ago quite accidentally one morning on a deep ship canal. After a biteless period I had stopped my retrieve purely to fumble in my pockets for a lighter, thus letting the fly sink well down along the near side drop-off.

Almost immediately upon continuing the retrieve, the fly was snatched by an eight-pounder. The trick was repeated several times in the next few casts, each pike intercepting the fly as it searched the bottom of the slope. The habit stuck – although thankfully I've ditched the cigarettes.

Rivers

From smallish tributaries to the big, famous waterways, pike thrive in just about every river suitable for coarse fish. Like drains, these waters regularly offer great potential for minimum expense and some of the fittest and most beautifully conditioned predators you will ever encounter. The other great advantage is that they don't freeze over and with their perpetual motion, river fish must often remain active throughout the winter months unlike their stillwater counterparts. It's never too cold for pike and on one morning last winter I had an action-packed session when the thermometer read -8°C.

Of all the different pike waters, however, rivers are also perhaps the most changeable of all, demanding a greater degree of watercraft and skill in presenting flies correctly. Knowing when as well as where to fish can be vital to success in running water.

Rains and the resulting extra colour can render even the most appetising river into a muddy soup in which nothing will be able to locate your fly. That said, a tinge of colour should not be feared and bigger, brighter flies may assist here. Settled conditions are your best bet and a particularly good period is when the river is fining down and clearing after a time of flood; following a period of poor visibility and sheltering from strong flows, the pike

The game becomes even more exciting when pike can be spotted and cast to. This spring fish was sitting in little more than a foot of water.

can suddenly feed with a vengeance.

Locating the areas likely to hold pike can be the easy part of river fishing. Look for any vantage point out of the main push of water. Slack areas, snags or obstructions which interrupt the flow are always worth investigation; deep pools and bends, undercut banks and submerged trees are all classic river pike territory here. On larger, more featureless rivers you may have to look harder to locate changes in depth and hidden obstructions and other features. Manmade structures such as weirs and flood relief arms also invariably hold predators.

There is a great deal to be said for 'learning' your chosen river. A walk with polarising glasses on a clear day when water levels are low and visibility

fine could save a lot of guesswork. Don't always expect the obvious either: my first-ever river pike came from a spot directly underneath the bank, a hole which I had probably walked past a dozen times as a child armed with a roach pole.

Another productive area was one of those swims where you might easily say to yourself 'but that's way too shallow to hold a pike.' It wasn't and in February the area contained some big females to over 20lb.

Perhaps the best way to proceed is to treat river piking as a grand game of hide-and-seek and one it may take you a fair investment of time to win. Instant fishing it often isn't, but the art of reading and remembering a particular water course is a fascinating, rewarding process.

This long, powerful river pike came from a deep slack area. The fish took a well-weighted fly presented on a fast intermediate line.

Getting the fly to the fish is another challenge in itself and it is no use whatsoever having the sexiest-looking pattern in the world if it is simply rushed through in the current, high and wide of any waiting predators. Pike are not as fussy as trout when it comes to presentation but it is vital to get the fly as close to a waiting attacker as possible. Unless fishing slower water therefore it is often best to cast upstream or up and across, so that the fly sinks and moves with the flow. Fish against the flow and in all but shallow water it may be simply pulled up in the water and out of the take zone. On slow, deep rivers you can also cast across and gently walk downstream with the flow to prevent such drag occurring.

An intermediate or sinking line is a great help here, especially where the water is deep. Our flies should also be tailored to running water. Unlike on stillwater, where we can simply wait for flies to sink to the required depth, rivers demand faster sinking patterns and it is well worth tying some weightier, sinking versions of favourite flies with heavier hooks or added lead wire to get down to the fish. Patterns with dumbbell eyes are particular favourites in this regard and scaled up versions of those in the sections on perch and zander are particularly effective. Failing this, I always have a container of tungsten putty in a pocket as a quick fix way of adding weight to a fly or leader in order to get down to the fish.

Accessibility can be another thorny issue worthy of mention for river anglers. A boat may be essential to fish some areas and a massive advantage on larger rivers such as the Thames or Severn. The majority of us are not boat owners however and we must access the water however possible. Waders can be a big help, especially on smaller rivers, but many of the stretches favourable to pike are too deep and treacherous to wade safely. Another solution to the problem of accessibility might be to use a salmon outfit and the long reach of a speycasting weapon to good effect.

The subject of river piking is a complex matter and it is worth reminding the reader that the sheer power of river pike shouldn't be underestimated. These creatures are far stronger than their lazier stillwater cousins and a good-sized specimen can pull back with a berserk power. With this in mind, 20lb plus fluorocarbon is recommended, along with a robust wire trace and a rod with

WEIGHTY MATTERS

Tungsten putty is an excellent way to increase quickly the sink rate of a fly, which can be essential in running water or very deep stillwaters. This can be moulded to the leader just in front of the fly or even added to the head. Unlike split shot, it won't kink the trace.

Predator fly expert Nigel Savage cradles a reservoir monster. The fish took a roach-coloured baitfish pattern of his own design (as featured at the end of this chapter).

some serious stopping power. If you glean nothing else from my notes here, do remember to tackle up accordingly for these river monsters, which will quickly discover any weakness in your tackle.

Lakes & Reservoirs

It says a great deal about the adaptability of pike that they can be found in so many different waters.

Lakes are no exception, from the largest, wildest loch down to smaller and more sedate manmade lakes. We also have the phenomenon of trout reservoir pike on Chew, Rutland and other large venues. It is perhaps no coincidence that these renowned flyfishing waters have proved to be one of the chief areas for a cross-fertilisation of ideas between the game and pike fraternities. The difference we find today is that rather than maligning pike as vermin, fly anglers are now recognising them as true 'sport' fish.

Larger lakes especially can present a daunting challenge for pike. Even with a boat at your disposal, location can be a far more pressing problem where you find acres of water – but the basic rules are the same; we must pick up the trail and every clue possible.

Visible features such as reed lines, bays, inlets and islands can be a good starting point. Prey fish may be hard to spot on any large breezy water, but grebes, cormorants, gulls and others indicate prey concentrations. However, many of the really important features and holding areas will be a good deal less obvious, much of the time hidden beyond sight. Depth changes are the perfect place to catch – whether we are talking about shelves, sudden drop-offs or even features such as the old river beds or submerged walls on reservoirs.

When compared to other methods (float fished deadbaits or heavy jigs for example) flyfishing is not a very efficient way of determining depths. Guesswork alone is no answer and thus maps, local anglers and other sources are all worth seeking out for obvious reasons.

Another useful tool is the dreaded fish-finder, maligned by traditionalists but a godsend for those scratching for clues on a large water. Deep troughs, shallow plateaux, submerged rocks or weedbeds: all can be vital areas you might not locate with a fly rod or the naked eye. Even where no such giveaways are found, it's helpful to note the depth: for example, if you find no fish in 6ft of water, try ten and so on... and when you do get a take, note the depth and any characteristics found. It's very easy to forget all details of depth counted down and how quickly you were retrieving in the excitement of a take but it really is always worth making mental notes.

As with all pike fishing, tackling big waters should be a mobile affair – and we should quickly dispel any notion that one only need cast a big ugly fly into a trout reservoir to succeed. When boat fishing, this often means drifting with a drogue to slow you down while you cover as much likely water as possible. The fish are

DEEP CONCERNS

Whichever type of lake you tackle, having a fair impression of the depth can be vital. Where a pocket of deep water exists in the midst of wider shallows is ideal – big pike often love these mixed areas and even on quite a bare lake, contours and slopes provide key areas for predators to lurk. I once learned this lesson the hard way, struggling on a Finnish lake where a seemingly extortionately priced trolling map turned out to be worth every euro; two deep depressions in the midst of acres of featureless, shallow water produced some cracking pike.

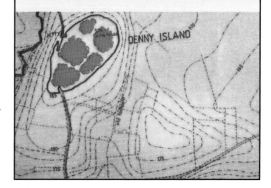

seldom evenly spread, but time and again they show in concentrations, sometimes with hectic action following long periods of inactivity.

In spite of my reservations about using those extra large, ugly-to-cast pike flies, on reservoirs and on other large waters where you want to give the pike the best possible chance to locate your pattern, they are highly useful. A fast intermediate line usually replaces the floater for me – it cuts through choppy water to be fished deeper if necessary, whilst a lively retrieve will still work in the shallows.

A key factor is the angle of the cast in relation to a drifting boat (see diagram): cast directly in front of a drifting boat, the flies lose momentum – just as when cast behind they may be pulled too high in the water. Cast to the side however, the fly will come round in a tantalising curve, just as trout anglers favour, the boat adding to and not hindering the presentation.

Organisation is also crucial for the boat angler – I like an unhooking mat ready on the deck, with net and unhooking tools to hand and all other gear neatly stowed away. Indeed, it is fatal to have too much clutter, as anything which may catch on your fly line around the boat could lead to disaster if a good fish is hooked.

Certain times of year are certainly more conducive to enjoyable flyfishing than others when faced with extensive acres to search. Published writing on the subject so far has also shown a real bias towards boat fishing and trout reservoirs, in my opinion. But the bank angler needn't feel left out and from gravel pits to wild lakes, the opportunities are there if you time it right. The obvious restriction is that of distance when casting – but at certain times, such as early morning feeding spells or when gathering to spawn early in the year, pike can be found in very shallow water. Such times offer tremendous potential for flyfishing – indeed, when wading there may be more risk of spooking the fish than there is of falling short on the cast.

Some days you wouldn't believe the fish are so close in until you almost trip over them. Well ahead of spring, and especially when rain water swells the shoreline to drown the banks, the pike will already be sizing up areas to gather in. On one lake,

BARBED, BARBLESS OR 'BUMPED'?

Debate still continues on the merits of barbless hooks – personally, I don't believe many more fish are lost on de-barbed hooks provided you maintain steady pressure. The best of both worlds, however, is to carefully crush the barb down to a bump – which should stay put but can be removed with no damage.

an overgrown gravel pit, I recall a cold day in February when several pike fell to a fly cast into no more than 3ft of water whilst other anglers were still launching sardines towards the horizon.

Waders can be excellent on overgrown banks to access tricky spots but a good rule is always to cast first and observe before plunging in: it is a myth that pike are afraid of nothing. Another big plus point of wading, especially for pike that may spawn in the near future, is that you needn't remove any fish caught, from the water. On many occasions the hook can be slipped out and the fish instantly returned with an absolute minimum of stress.

Above: Ice on the rod tip: but still every chance of action.

Below: No matter how cold it gets, pike will still take a fly.

Float Tubing

There are more types of pike flyfishing than there is space in an entire book, let alone one chapter – but as a final point it is worth touching on one area of the sport which is possibly the most exciting of all: Float tubing. This is a superbly effective way to fish. Whilst you cannot travel the same distances you might with a motor, tubing has several advantages over boat fishing. In spite of the ungainly appearance, it affords a great deal of control and surprising stability, coming into its own in spring and early summer when the fish are lying inshore. With the average float tube sitting comfortably inside a suitcase, they are brilliant for the travelling angler, a godsend for all those destinations where boat hire isn't possible or bank fishing is limited.

Paddling stealthily in the tube, it is possible to get close to the pike without spooking them, searching all those nooks and crannies so awkward to boat and bank anglers. It's tricky to cast especially far but the truth is you simply won't need to. Indeed, some of the most exciting pike flyfishing I have ever experienced

Have tube, will travel: the author explores a Scandinavian lake. Float tubes are not only portable, but are a great way to get up close and personal with pike in awkward areas.

has been by tube, flicking poppers close to cover and witnessing incredible takes at close quarters. Tubing comes highly recommended – just take a change of underwear for that moment when a metre long pike follows the fly right to your toes! (For more on float tubing see: www. dgfishing.co.uk)

Pike Traces

A wire trace is essential for pike flyfishing. These are typically 1ft or more (and I prefer 16in) of flexible wire. Lighter, knottable wires (such as Surflon or Proleader) are ideal for smaller scale pike angling, but for big flies and hefty casts, a heavier, multi-

UNHOOKING AND RELEASING PIKE

With numerous teeth and a mean appearance, pike can be a daunting prospect. In reality however, they are fragile fish that won't bite you and demand care on the bank. With a few simple, sound guidelines, both you and esox should remain unscathed!

1. The first essential to good handling happens before you ever hook the fish, with your own preparation. Keep unhooking tools, scales etc where they can be instantly and easily located and accessed.
2. Control the fish. Before you attempt to retrieve the fly, make sure you are in charge. The pike should be lain on an unhooking mat, or wet grass at the very least. If the fish thrashes, simply hold it firmly in place.
3. With the fish under control, locate the fish's gill plates on the underside of the head. If unsure, you might want to wear a glove.
4. Run your index finger along the inside of the gill plate, taking care not to catch the red gill rakers.
5. Once you reach the front of the jaw you'll find a softish area with no teeth to grab. The mouth should open fairly easily. Remove the fly with an appropriate tool (*see illustration*).
6. If you want to weigh or photograph the fish, you should do so as quickly as possible – and you could even give the fish a breather by holding it upright in the water within the landing net head.
7. Now for release. Never carry a fish back to the water in your hands – if you drop it, this could be fatal. Bring it in the net, or held snugly in an unhooking mat. Now hold the fish upright in the water. Wait until the fish is ready and swims off of its own accord.

strand wire is advisable (Greys Prowla, ET 49 Strand).

At one end of the trace is a small but strong snap link, as used by the lure angler; at the other end a rig ring (simply a metallic oval or circle – see picture) to attach the trace to your leader. I usually find swivels

unnecessary, although a quality rolling swivel can add some movement to a big fly. Whatever your choice NEVER knot wire directly on to fishing line – this is suicidal!

Followers & Takers

Fairly common, sometimes frustrating behaviour with pike is the tendency to follow the fly but refuse to take. So what are the choices? Slowing down the retrieve can give the fish too long to study the fly; and besides, do fleeing prey fish slow down when being harried? Speeding up the retrieve often works better – although you then run the risk of the pike giving up pursuit. The best response I believe is to try to trigger a reaction, which usually means pausing to let the fish catch up before making the fly accelerate forward as if escaping. You can't win them all, but you'll get more hits by forcing the pike to make a decision.

Casting Pike Flies

Casting a big fly on a nine weight or greater set-up demands a different approach. Predator rods tend to have a slower action; hence a slightly slower casting action is advisable. Line speed is important with heavy flies, and double haul casts are useful to prevent the fly from dropping in flight. Another handy piece of advice for those starting out is to avoid monstrous flies for initial efforts – try a more modest fly (no bigger than 1/0) at first on an 8 or 9 weight outfit and get

HOW BIG SHOULD PIKE FLIES BE?

It is something of a myth that pike flies need to be huge. On small waters especially, something in the 2-3in range can be effective and much more pleasant to cast. Research shows that pike are generally opportunists rather than feeders which 'select' big fish. In coloured conditions or when searching acres of water however, a big fly might be easier to locate for the pike.

a feel for it. This is far less of a jump from casting trout lures and you can always step up as you get more comfortable.

Sink Tips

Besides the option of full sinking or inter-mediate lines, sinking poly-leaders offer a quicker solution to getting the fly deeper. These can be attached to a floating line in seconds as required. Go for the most robust you can find (ie salmon or tarpon).

Drifting with a Drogue

Using a drogue to drift a breezy lake is an ideal way to cover the water. Drogues should always be fastened to two points on the boat to give a parachute effect. Note the position of the drogue itself. Sideways casts, as shown, allow pike flies to be assisted by the drift, swinging round in an attractive arc. For slower drifts and on blustery days, you might try attaching the drogue to the stern. *(See diagram on page 61)*

Steve Moore enjoys a healthy scrap with a large pike on Chew Reservoir.

PIKE FLIES

FROST BITE

FIRE STARTER

Hook: Sakuma Phantom, Size 1
Thread: Dark Kevlar
Body: White EP fibres, pearl krystal flash
Barred sides: Grizzle Cock
Cheeks: Hot orange chickabou
Head: Pinch of black deer hair or bucktail
Eyes: Holographic eyes (Deer Creek), epoxied in place

Pike flies needn't always be huge. This pattern is excellent for canal and drain fishing and has a bit of everything: light and dark, some sparkle and a prominent 'hot spot'. Bucktail makes for a durable head – or alternatively deer hair makes for a slower sinker which is ideal where half the water depth may be choked with weed. A good sized all-rounder, this can be presented comfortably on an eight weight. For tying instructions see 'Really Useful Flies' (page 201).

Hook: Sakuma Phantom, Size 1–1/0
Thread: Dark Kevlar
Body: Pearl mylar tube over thread/lead wire
Back & Tail: Barred Zonker Strip
Hot Spot: Jungle cock or yellow (optional)
Head: 3D eyes, fixed with epoxy

Rabbit fur is a superb material for pike flies. Not only do zonker style flies wiggle beautifully, the material adds a real push and movement to the fly. Brightly coloured patterns can provoke an aggressive response when more natural shades aren't working. The sparkling throat of the fly is created by simply folding the frayed ends of the mylar tubing under the hook and securing with thread.

PIKE FLIES

BLACK EMPEROR

SUPER TINSEL

Hook: Sakuma Manta, 1/0–5/0
Thread: Black
Tail: EP fibres, black 3D
Body: Black chenille or any coarse black dubbing
Rib: Dark red or green wire
Hackle: Large black game hackle
Cheeks (optional): Jungle Cock
Head: Built up thread, with holographic eyes epoxied on

This supersized woolly bugger is a good option for clear water and cold conditions. Never underestimate black as a colour for pike – it can work when the rest don't.

Hook: Sakuma Manta, 1–5/0
Thread: Kevlar
Body/Wing: Tinsel in any colour, blended with few bright coloured synthetic fibres
Head: Epoxy & Holo Eyes

Subtle it isn't, but every pike fly box should include a few bright and flashy numbers. You can blend different tinsels and fibres to get your own special effects; try pink, red or iridescent blue. This one shouldn't stay looking glamorous for too long once the jaws arrive!

Besides fish imitations, weedless deer hair flies, and artificial mice – deer hair frog patterns can provide great pike-fishing sport, especially if you have to work your way around lily pads and similar heavy weed cover.

SAVAGE'S BAITFISH

PIKE POPPERS

Hook: Sakuma Manta 1/0–5/0
Thread: Kevlar
Body: EP Fibres or Llama Hair in suitable colours (white, black, dark blue, olive) plus a few strands of Krystal Flash or similar
Fins: Hot orange fibres
Head: Wader glue (eg 'Storm Sure'), 3D eyes (Deer Creek)
Target Spot (optional): Black or red holographic sequins

This fantastic baitfish pattern is named after its maker, Rutland Warden, and predator expert Nigel Savage (who is so modest he'll probably slap me for naming this fly after him). A few clever key features distinguish this from the rest. Firstly, the fly is tied part way down the shank in the style of a big saltwater pattern, which avoids those annoying wrap-rounds encountered with big flies where the body material twists around the hook. The other notable feature is the realistically profiled head, which is shaped using a good smear of wader glue. Not only does this increase durability, it

Hook: Special longshank model 1/0–3/0
Thread: Kevlar
Main Body: Preformed popper body, painted & well varnished
Dressing: Large game hackles in desired colour
Tail: Two strips of zonker, plus strands of flash material

Nothing makes the heart race quite like fishing a surface popper. Bodies are now widely available which can easily be painted and customised with your own materials. Perhaps the best colour is black, which shows up superbly against a light surface. Fish with jerky pulls and brief pauses.

THE ART OF POPPING

Savage's Baitfish continued...
also gives the fly a more realistic profile and increases resistance, therefore adding movement. Sequins and other adornments are optional – the barred perch markings are simply done with a pantone marker or sharpie pen.

Mild evenings are the perfect time to work a popper in shallow water. A scene which is unlikely to remain calm for too long.

'Popping' – or the art of creating a wake with a floating fly across the surface of a water, is one of the genuine highlights of the pike angler's year. At its best in spring and early summer, a healthy-sized buoyant fly can bring the sort of sport to make your jaw drop and your heart lurch.

On certain waters and times of year it proves ineffectual: when the fish are sulking on the bottom of a deep lake in autumn, for example. But when pike are holding near to the shore in spring or loitering around cover in the summer, it can be devilishly good.

A beefy set-up, say a 10-11 weight, is best if you like a large popper, both because of the size and weight of flies and also the likelihood of having to wrestle with pike close to snags and cover. Strong fluorocarbon tends to drag the fly under the surface so I usually swap this for a length of heavy, floating mono.

Two further points should be briefly made about poppers. Firstly, they seem able to attract a good stamp of pike. Does the commotion of a bulging surface lure suggest a prey item far bigger than the actual target? Secondly, the extra shock-waves kicked out by a popping or waking fly add a greater presence than subsurface flies. For this reason, poppers and the like can be very useful in coloured water where they prove easier for pike to locate than many sinking flies, which tend to disappear.

How should a popper be fished? A steady series of jerky pulls is usually the way, punctuated by little pauses. When casting close to a likely lie, a good tip is to wait at least ten seconds after the 'plop' of the fly, to let any nearby monster home in on it. A fairly continuous retrieve can work well in open water, but around cover such as lilies and duck weed you can throw in a lot more pauses to give a 'stop-start' retrieve. This gives the impression of a small frog or rodent twitching around the cover – and pike will literally bash their way through vegetation in order to grab a free meal. Weedless flies are useful here – sometimes vital. When pike grab a fly through cover, they seem to take a second longer to engulf the target, so if your nerves can stand it, it's therefore often best to allow a split second or two before striking to let the pike seize and turn with the fly. Open water is more straightforward, although it's not unusual to miss as many bites as you connect with, as your popper is smashed. Don't forget to bring strong leaders – and a change of underpants!

A relaxed casting style and adequate gear are required for pike flies and even more so for bulky artificial poppers.
A controlled haul with the line hand helps everything straighten out.

Do Eyes and Hotspots make any Difference?

Bright fins and target markings are optional but I believe such 'target points' really add to the effectiveness of a fly. Some may disagree, but what is certain is that a well-finished fly brings confidence.

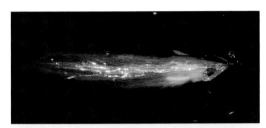

Even the more natural-looking flies are boosted by some added colour and flash.

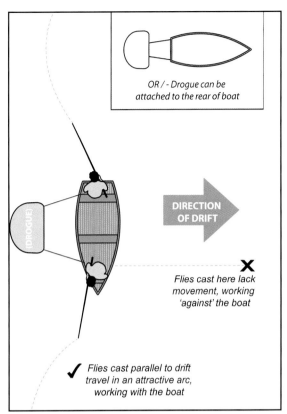

OR / - Drogue can be attached to the rear of boat

(DROGUE)

DIRECTION OF DRIFT

X
Flies cast here lack movement, working 'against' the boat

✓ *Flies cast parallel to drift travel in an attractive arc, working with the boat*

Above: Using a drogue to get an attractive fly presentation when drifting for pike.

Below: Boats moored in readiness at Chew.

This 3lb 2oz fish was
sitting on the drop-off
on a ship canal in
some 10ft of water.
The author took it on a
sunny day on a jig fly.

PERCH

With handsome looks, a keen eye and a big mouth, the perch is the gentleman thug of the coarse fishes; he's also arguably the most under-rated species of all for the flyfisher. Found just about everywhere from the most uninspiring little drain to the biggest loch, this attractive predator will take a fly with gusto.

The little ones can be recklessly bold, the larger fish surprisingly wily; either way, the perch provides an accessible and obliging quarry.

A great shame therefore that so few of us would ever fish deliberately for them with game tackle, since excellent results have followed for those few enthusiasts to give it a try.

Perhaps tellingly, in the seminal work *Stillwater Angling* Dick Walker himself considered that a suitably-dressed fly was perhaps the deadliest method of all for perch. And with good reason: a fly possesses superb movement in the water and yet can also be presented a great deal slower than the time-honoured Mepps spinner. Perch are also well-known for their tendency to 'nip' the tail of conventional hard-bodied lures, whereas at other times even a fair-sized fly is quite effortlessly sucked in whole.

PERCH TACKLE & SEASON

TACKLE: In waters where perch are the only major predator, an outfit as light as a 4/5wt may suffice. In common practice however, an 8wt is the safer option to handle the inevitable pike attacks and also allow the casting of larger flies. Floating line will handle shallow stillwaters and rivers up to around 6ft, but intermediate or sinking lines may be vital for deeper venues and fast sink lines may be required for reservoir fishing.

Leaders: If no pike are present, 8-10ft of 8lb fluorocarbon will suffice. However, if pike are a risk, it is unwise to fish lighter than 12lb fluorocarbon with a fine wire trace as insurance.

Other: Forceps, long-handled landing net.

SEASON: Perch can be caught year round, but the cooler months from Sept-April are traditional favourites. My biggest perch have come in March and April. Summer fishing is also viable but warm water and extensive weed growth can make for added difficulties.

Perch School

My own adventures with perch on the fly began in the humble setting of small canals and rivers. The location of perch, as any small boy will testify, can be utterly predictable. As all the textbooks declare, they are great lovers of structure: sunken trees and posts; bridges, boats and bushes.

On slower days, whilst pike fishing for example, I would happily run a trout lure around walls and sunken obstacles purely to watch gangs of these boldly-striped attackers dart out and grab the fly. I have to admit that I still find the exercise a gratifying diversion on a slow, sunny day when I can happily regress to being twelve years old again.

Besides the obvious safety and concealment of natural or manmade structures, it seems that perch also like the shade they provide. In fact, my first good-sized perch came from learning this lesson in less than idyllic surroundings, partly by sheer chance.

On a bright autumn afternoon with few bites, I had been idly trailing a pike fly along a wall beneath a motorway bridge. Just where the well-lit water tailed off into darkness, the line suddenly bumped and jarred solid. The juddering fight immediately suggested no jack pike and after several plunging runs in the shade of the bridge, out sailed a splendid, broad-barred perch.

A cracking reservoir perch for Sam Edmonds, the result of finding the fish and presenting a suitable lure at the right depth. Concentrations of autumn fry don't just catch the eye of resident trout.

Small perch will also take nymphs. This one came from a tiny stream.

There is always something special about a solid perch: the arched back, those brilliant orangey red fins and that huge caricature of a mouth. For the next few hours the pike fishing was hastily abandoned and in the following weeks and months I began dreaming up some more suitable perch flies for future trips.

From Big Bites to Fussy Feeders

You may be unlikely to catch the perch of a lifetime from a small waterway, but it is here, in these clear, weedy surroundings that you will find the best possible apprenticeship in the art of perch fishing. Indeed, simply watching how perch behave and the manner in which they respond to a fly is a worthwhile pursuit.

The habits of perch are notable for their sheer variation and they are always an intriguing quarry. To my mind, they resemble some of the dodgier human characters loitering in a small town. The young fish move in definite gangs of similar-sized fish, whereas the older and bigger fish may be found in smaller groups or even alone. This accounts partly for the variable behaviour of the species. The little ones are competitive and greedy- life

is about capitalising on food and growing quicker than their shoal mates. They can be bold to the point of fearlessness, eagerly pursuing and snapping up their quarry.

The larger fish are anything but stupid, forming definite habits and feeding with more caution. Like large pike or trout, they will command the best, safest lies and most suitable feeding areas and our best guide to location will be not only a matter of cover and depth, but of proximity to a good supply of food. Indeed, some of my biggest perch have come from seemingly featureless areas, the only real giveaway being concentrations of small roach.

Diet varies, but while small-to-medium sized perch will take anything from damsel nymphs to tadpoles (bizarrely I've even caught tiddlers on Pheasant Tail nymphs), the bigger fish are those which thrive on other fish, ranging from roach and dace, to bleak and gudgeon. Some detective work will also reveal other lines of enquiry. Many canals and drains teem with small, dark 'motherless minnows' which may form the staple diet. Elsewhere, many rivers and lakes have become colonised by crayfish. These waters, by no coincidence, often yield huge perch and, who knows, the adaptable flyfisher armed with some suitable patterns could catch some stupendously chunky specimens.

Perch Fly Patterns

Very few fly patterns have emerged specifically for perch. Most are taken on trout or pike flies, but to my mind existing patterns are less than ideal. Pike flies are rather too large, trout lures perhaps not quite meaty enough for such a big mouth. A happy medium seems to be a hook size from 1-4, and besides the patterns suggested in these pages, you may well want to adapt your own lures from existing favourites. Trout lures, for example, can be scaled up a notch or two.

The challenge of getting perch to take a fly is not always straightforward, especially if the fish are big or wary. Perch feed rather differently to other predators, lacking the speed and ferocity of pike. Sometimes they will nip at a fly and it is not unusual to feel plucks on the line. Perch have been observed chasing and harrying smaller fish, disabling them first before swallowing helpless prey whole. With this in mind, it is important to use the sharpest of hooks and avoid overdressing flies or using long, trailing tails.

Retrieves

Speed of retrieve can be absolutely crucial to success. Actively hunting perch will take a fast-moving fly, but on many other occasions they need time to react. Race a fly too quickly past the fish and Mr Perch may quickly abandon pursuit – or not bother in the first place. Move your fly too slowly, on the other hand, and you may give the fish too much time to study the fly. Above all we want the fish to react, providing the stimulus but also enough time to make a grab. It is a matter of experimentation: a busy yet not over-hurried retrieve is usually the best answer. Again, if you get the chance to fish for perch at close quarters and observe the response in clear water, this is excellent practise.

This chunky winter perch came from a one-acre pond. As winter temperatures drop, even murky waters can clear, offering great fly rod sport.

Chris Gooding takes aim at a perchy-looking tree line. Deeper areas with some cover are prime habitat.

Big or small, perch are always pretty. A fish to help you rediscover your inner twelve-year-old.

Fly Line & Colours

Fly line choice can be very important in perch fishing. Floaters are fine for water of up to 6ft in depth, but any deeper and you would be advised to try an intermediate or sinker. The problem is often that with floating or very slow sinking lines, you may be able to sink the fly deep enough initially but it will quickly be drawn up and out of the perch's window of attack on the retrieve. Sink tips are another useful addition to keep your fly deeper, where it is likely to be taken.

Is fly colour an important factor in perch flies? Some would say not, but white or silver seem to be excellent, as is yellow or sometimes black. I also like to mix some red into my patterns. For some reason perch pick out red very well and it has been proved that perch see colours in the red part of the spectrum exceptionally well. A 'hot spot' can also make your fly easier to pick out in low light or coloured water, while it's also notable that prey fish such as roach and juvenile perch have red fins. Whatever the reason, it's revealing just how many favourite traditional perch lures such as spinners also sport a tuft of red wool.

Big Mouth Strikes Again

In my mind's eye, I can still picture a trio of supremely big, gruesome perch I spotted one autumn morning. As I write this they are no doubt sitting in their usual spot, three hulking, striped yobs unnoticed by

passing dog-walkers. These brutes hug the shady centre of perhaps a 30yd stretch of snaggy water. In the lighter margins you can spot their little brothers and sisters in the shallows, loitering where shoals of roach and rudd pass rather nervously. You can catch the little perch for fun here – but the big bullies are another story. If you cast to these monsters on a sunny, still afternoon, the response is one of total apathy. No fools, these three. After a dozen casts you might wonder if they're alive at all. But if you arrive at first light, or on a dull, breezy day when fry are moving, these muggers come to life. It is during these short spells that a lively fly might just work, when you might witness a set of thick, jail-bar stripes moving and the sudden disappearance of your artificial inside a wide, murderous mouth. I've caught one of these three thugs and, who knows, perhaps one day the biggest of this bad bunch will take a fly?

On other waters, the action is less visual but the perch are equally impressive, sometimes bigger still. There are countless stillwaters with big perch lurking; sadly for the fly caster, many day ticket and club waters are also characterised by greedy carp and the ensuing murky, churned-up water they create. Just occasionally however, when the chill of winter clears the water and the fair weather fishers thin out, you may find the right conditions to cast a fly and every chance of a fat, well-fed perch.

This urban perch was sitting underneath a concrete walkway. It quickly dashed out to grasp a fly jigged right under the rod tip.

If you seek even greater monsters, the much larger waters are probably the answer. Many of our bigger trout reservoirs hold giants which occasionally surprise visiting pike anglers or snatch lures intended for trout. But with a dedicated approach, the adventurous fly angler might discover some sensational perch fishing. Rutland, Chew, Grafham and many other lakes have yielded great numbers of large perch and some outstanding specimens to over 4lb. Grand, wild waters such as Scotland's lochs and the waters of the Lake District also have their hidden surprises.

Tactics for these big water beasts are very different to those for shallow rivers and drains. For much of the year, sinking lines are a must and the colder the temperature gets, the more the perch will retreat into the depths. Otherwise, the usual structures are all worthy of investigation: from buoys to boat yards, and even trout cages. Areas where the bank drops off steeply into deeper water are also particularly good to investigate. Trout fishers sometimes contact the resident perch by accident, but targeting these fish by design with suitably scaled-up reservoir favourites such as Minkies and Boobies could yield some fine perch.

It's also worth noting that surface popping flies have been used with some success by fly casters for perch. Many of the flies employed by US bass anglers might be given a fair trial – albeit scaled down a little. I've only rarely enjoyed success with floating patterns, but undoubtedly

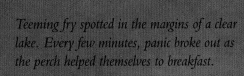

Teeming fry spotted in the margins of a clear lake. Every few minutes, panic broke out as the perch helped themselves to breakfast.

ONE FLY OR A SHOAL?

Trout fishermen often present a team of nymphs, so why not a little 'shoal' of fry patterns? Three or four small fry flies can easily be presented together. My favourite 'small fry' are simply made with light lure hooks, silver bodies and a light wing of arctic runner and krystal flash. A slightly larger fly on the point will help straighten the team out.

You may even take multiple perch on one cast! The only major objection is the presence of pike however – which will easily bite through 10lb fluorocarbon.

the method can and does work on waters where perch venture into shallow water to hit prey on or just under the surface. The only largish perch I've ever landed on a Popper came on a wild, boggy lake in Finland. Did the presence of hundreds of juvenile frogs have anything to do with this I wonder? The perch lurking in the overgrown corners of the place were quick to latch onto anything kicking its way around the edge.

Wherever you live, the chances are you'll find perch-fishing possibilities. Perhaps the sad truth is that most anglers are simply not interested in perch if trout or pike are on offer. Never mind: this is good news for perch lovers, as the species thrives on neglect. Buck the usual trends and with a dedicated approach you might find a great deal more than the occasional 'accidental' specimen.

71

PERCH FLIES

PERCH SPECIAL

Hook: Long shank lure 2-8
Tail: Tuft of red wool
Body: Flat silver tinsel, ribbed with silver wire
Wing: White marabou fibres mixed with angel hair or similar flashy material
Head: Holographic eyes, over black thread

This is a reliable clear water pattern to mimic fingerling roach, offering wiggle, flash and a classic red target point.

JIG FLY

Hook: Size 2-6 Lure
Head: Dumbbell eyes, tied to underside of hook, Clouser-style
Tail: Bright EP or synthetic fibres with a few strands of flash material
Body: Fritz or bright synthetic dubbing
Collar: Grizzle hackle

Dumbbell head flies designed to fish hookpoint up are especially useful in deep or cold water. The up and down motion of such designs is also deadly for perch, offering plenty of motion even at slow speed, rather like a jig. This pattern has accounted for my biggest perch to date.

HANNINGFIELD LURE

Hooks: Two size 8s joined securely by fine pike wire
Bodies: White ice dubbing (orig. wool)
Tail: Chickabou (orig: hot orange hackle, wound round)
Rib: Silver oval tinsel
Front Throat Hackle: Hot orange
Rear Throat Hackle: Short, bright blue
Wing: Arctic fox, krystal flash & duck (orig: goat & turkey)
Cheeks: Jungle Cock

This is my own tying of Richard Walker's classic perch fly. He originally devised this pattern for trout – but quickly discovered it was even deadlier for perch. Besides adding extra wiggle, the jointed rear hook is useful for hooking predators nipping at tails. Modern materials can help spruce up an already fine design. I like the colour and movement of holographic materials & 'chickabou' for tails. For those old sticklers however, the original materials are given in brackets where I've taken liberties.

ZANDER

On first impressions, the zander might seem a strange choice of quarry for the fly caster. They quite often favour murky water. The species also hugs the depths for much of the time, thus virtually ruling out sight-fishing. Add in their patchy distribution and even patchier notes on flyfishing for them and most anglers don't bother. But this is a great shame when you consider the merits of this fascinating species.

For one thing, zander have excellent eyesight even in low light levels, and can locate a fly more easily than might be imagined. The fly approach can also provide a consistently slow, deep presentation for these unseen attackers, with fast sink lines and special flies well suited to the job. Stillwaters such as Grafham have certainly demonstrated the potential of flyfishing, with some huge fish taken by enterprising anglers. And in spite of a reputation as a poor fighter, zander perform surprisingly well on light tackle. Once again, it is another case of where it is not the effectiveness of flyfishing which is the barrier – but a lack of willingness on the part of anglers to try.

In short, the zander is a worthwhile possibility on game tackle and slowly but surely, specialist zander tactics are emerging from a handful of experts. On this subject, I am grateful to Nigel Savage, without whose guidance my own grounding in zander flyfishing would be much poorer.

ZANDER TACKLE & SEASON

TACKLE: Zander may lack the fight of larger predators, but you still require fairly robust tackle to cast large flies and deal with accidentally hooked pike! An 8wt outfit feels about right – although you could go as high as a ten for big flies, often with intermediate or sinking lines to get down to this deep-lying species.

Leaders: Should be similar to those for pike: 8-10ft of tough 12lb or greater fluorocarbon plus a tooth-proof wire trace.

Other: A pair of quality, long forceps or long-nosed pliers, a sensibly large landing net. Don't forget a head torch if you intend to stay late.

SEASON: September to March typically.

Is night fishing a must for zander? Not always – but low light is recommended. This school fish took in the last hour of light.

A Date with Dracula

For the unacquainted, the zander is a unique species with its own idiosyncrasies. Sometimes inaccurately called the 'pike perch' it does nevertheless share characteristics with both. It has fewer teeth than the pike, but a fantastically sinister dentistry including a pair of prey-crippling fangs Christopher Lee would be proud of: hence wire traces are vital. Along with the perch it shares a striking banner of a spiny dorsal fin and a characteristically slow, bludgeoning, head-shaking fight when hooked. Its origins in

Britain are often illegal in many areas; but like other late arrivals it has adapted with great success and after initial upheavals in various river and canal habitats, the species has reached balanced population levels. As with pike, however, there are still some ill-educated individuals who see them as vermin.

The zander has its own distinct habits, but it must be said they are often misunderstood. Perhaps the oldest myth is that you should fish at night. Whilst it's true that evenings are generally good and zander can indeed be caught after dark, plenty are caught in broad daylight too.

Certainly, I've caught the odd fish on a sunny afternoon.

The Challenge of Zander

That zander are trickier to locate and catch than pike is a fact. Their spread can be far patchier, and they are less solitary with the smaller 'school' zander forming groups. As a result you might search for hours on end without a touch only to find several zander in a small area. On drains and canals especially, they can be frustratingly nomadic although certain holding areas are always worth investigation: deeper areas, bridges, boatyards and spots where different channels intersect are all places likely to hold prey fish if not zander – and the zander may well move in to feed at some point.

In contrast to wide-roving pike anglers, I know several keen lure men who will simply pick a known vantage point and keep working an area until the zander arrive. With this idea, I can picture in my mind a perfect little zander spot on the narrow channel between two Scandinavian lakes – as the only access point between two bodies of water you can be sure that at some point fish will pass through.

Another key characteristic seems to be that zander like deeper water than pike. 'Drop offs' where shallow and deep water meet can be key on any venue and often form patrol routes for these predators. For much of their existence, zander are bottom hugging fish – hence a deeply presented fly is often essential.

It is only in low light and for short spells that they seem to maraud the upper layers of the water to send prey fish scattering – and in these short feeding spells a shallower, more vigorously-presented fly might score. For most of the time however, zander flyfishing is about

A fly rod in the Fens:
Nigel Savage searches for zander.

fishing the depths efficiently.

A notable remark of all the zander experts I have met is that I cannot remember any of them recalling a zander take witnessed first hand. They won't follow a fly over any distance as pike do for example. And indeed, whilst a hungry pike may rush several feet upwards to grab a fly, zander more often require a fly presented close to their chosen level in the water. In actual fact, zander flyfishers and especially those on stillwater can glean a great deal from jig fishermen, who present their lures in a slow and controlled manner, jigging artificials just off the bottom.

Flies and Presentations

The flies zander will take are manifold, but where do we start? For clear, relatively shallow waters such as drains, a 'match the hatch' approach can work well. Typical fodder are fishes such as roach and bleak. With smaller mouths, zander can't manage as large prey as pike but will still comfortably engulf a pike-sized fly. When you stop to consider it even quite a fairly large sized pattern may only be the size of a 1oz roach. Indeed, the beauty of a fly is that it is easy to suck in whole, and you shouldn't get as many frustrating taps as the jig fisher who feels the zander continuously knocking the tail of the lure.

That said, zander won't always hook themselves and any gentle taps or any unusual indications should be quickly met by a firm pull on the fly line.

For much of the time though, zander flies bear more in common with Clouser-style patterns or indeed jigs than pike flies. Natural isn't always best and in the muddier waters of rivers such as the Trent and Severn for example, bright yellows, oranges and pinks have found favour. Dumb-bell type heads are ideal for getting flies down to the bottom in flowing water and flies tied Clouser-style (hook point upwards) are well suited to the job. Not only do these snag less often but the up and down motion of a well-weighted fly is attractive in itself.

Most of my own success with zander has come on these snaggy, challenging rivers, which can look far from promising until you catch that first zander! Conditions are all-important where water levels and visibility can vary dramatically, and a clear or falling river is best. Settled spells of cold, dry weather will also help to clear the water and help our cause. The zander are invariably caught deep, often where the margins slope off into the main 'track' of the river.

A further word on visibility however: not only do zander have excellent eyesight, they positively thrive in low light conditions and poor visibility, when their superior senses help them hunt. Water like soup is not conducive to good flyfishing, but less than perfect visibility needn't be feared. You need to tailor your approach to coloured water, using bright colours and searching the water more thoroughly, or making more casts than you usually might in areas you know. The innovative tyer can really go to work here too and flies with rattle chambers, small spinning blades or other added vibration are all worthy of a fair trial.

This also leads us to perhaps the

RIVER FISHING FOR ZANDER

For the river angler, the challenge with zander is to present the fly just off the bottom, without the current lifting our pattern out of the take zone. From the bank, the best way is by casting out and across, just upstream. The fly presented thus, will sink and swing round attractively in the flow, and you can also walk downstream to prevent the fly overtaking you and the current lifting it up too high. A modest sinking line (such as a fast intermediate) and a well-weighted fly make an ideal combination for this task.

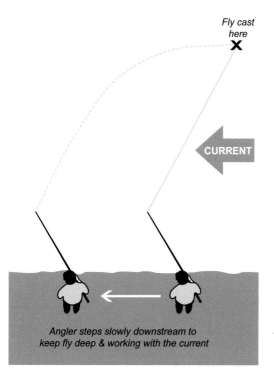

Fly cast here
X

CURRENT

Angler steps slowly downstream to keep fly deep & working with the current

most fascinating area of all: night fishing for zander. Beyond my own dabblings, pioneers such as Nigel Savage have landed zander well into darkness and besides the earlier suggestions, experiments with luminous flies such as my Night-watchman may yield interesting results. It's unlikely to replace the thrill of sea trout fishing but there is a definite, sinister buzz about the prospect of a sudden bite in the dark as a predator mauls your fly.

Into the Deep: Large Stillwaters

Besides drains, rivers and canals, the real headline-stealing zander caught on game tackle so far have been taken on large stillwaters, in particular reservoirs such as Grafham and Rutland. The tactics of flyfishers on these waters simply couldn't be more different however, and are in a sense more akin to the world of the jig fisherman than the river flyfisher.

Fast sink lines and fish finders are the order of the day in these often very deep waters, where boat anglers seek contours, troughs and other potential holding areas. It is not a case of repeated casting so much as drifting or 'trailing' a suitably-sized fly on these vast waters, to cover as many fish as possible.

An ultra-fast sink line such as a di-7 is a suitable tool for the job. Savvy anglers even use lines marked at regular intervals with silk whipping to carefully match the depth, whilst at the business end, a jig-style fly is presented on the bottom and gently tweaked to rise and pulse just off the deck.

Takes are detected by touch, with the angler pulling tight at any suspicious movement on the line.

Granted, it may be a less than elegant method, but it is one of the only effective ways to fish twenty plus feet of water effectively. A fish finder is seen as essential by most proponents in order to fish at the correct depth and to locate suitable areas and features as opposed to locating fish. Perhaps not a method for the purists then, but there is undoubtedly a strange and undeniable kick from hooking and playing a fish from way, way down in the depths and feeling the leaden thump of a decent fish on a full sinking line.

The safe return of fish landed from such chasms is a contentious issue in its own right. Various ideas have been mooted, including devices to sink the fish back down to a comfortable level post haste, for just like perch, zander are not the hardiest of fish. They may struggle to adjust to great depth changes and should be released as quickly as possible.

The issues of coloured water and feeding times have already been raised, but in brief, it seems the more coloured or deep the water, the less you need to fish into evening or night time. That said, some

sessions on vast, fairly clear lakes overseas have signalled the opposite trend during some of my fishing trips abroad. Working the depths for hours on a summer's day, you might think there were no fish in the lake. The fish are almost certainly lying deep and dormant, but not feeding. Have a cast at ten o'clock at night as the light is dying and it is a very different story, with the zander waking from their slumber and chasing small fish close to the shore-line. Suddenly it can be 'game on', with takes in only a metre or two of water. Such large bodies of water can be tough however, unless you know a water well or arrive with a few strong clues.

Zander are an exciting challenge. Sometimes hard to locate, let alone to catch: and one day's fishing can vary spectacularly from the next. This is equally

Zander o'clock! Unsocial hours can pay off where daytime sport is slow. Indeed, some specialists catch fish into darkness.

true of lure or bait fishing however. Persistence can be as vital, as can any cunning ideas you get. Perhaps this is what makes that moment of contact so special. Then, all the speculation ends, there is a solid knock on the line and the rod thumps over in sinister fashion.

A Fenland beast for Nigel Savage. This one hit a fly worked deep on the far shelf of a drain.

Hybrid Lures

Besides the pulse of tying materials, stronger vibration can be added to zander weapons in the form of soft grub tails and the like to create 'hybrid' flies.

ZANDER FLY INNOVATIONS

Zander flies are a fairly recent development, but are quickly falling into a class of their own. Where visibility and greater depths are an issue, several innovative features might make all the difference in the hunt for zander. Here are a few tips and tricks:

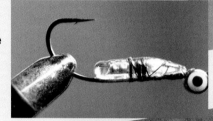

Rattles
A rattle is an excellent idea where the fish might need some extra help to locate the fly. The best of these are made of glass and highly audible. They should be tied in with the addition of epoxy, before the main body or wing of the fly is added.

Cones & Beads
Another way of getting an audible 'click' for fish to home in on is with the use of two sliding cone heads which are put on the shank between the eye and the main dressing to slide freely, as in this Nigel Savage pattern.

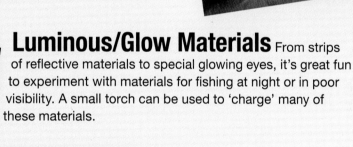

Luminous/Glow Materials
From strips of reflective materials to special glowing eyes, it's great fun to experiment with materials for fishing at night or in poor visibility. A small torch can be used to 'charge' many of these materials.

Graveyard Flies
Of all the snag-ridden horror swims I've fished, some of the worst have been zander spots on places like the River Severn. Where losses are high, I include a few flies tied on black Aberdeen hooks. With steady pressure and strong fluorocarbon, these simply bend out of trouble. They're still strong enough to land zander, which don't fight as hard as pike – and this way you won't be littering the bottom with lost flies.

ZANDER FLIES

JIG FLY

Hook: Sakuma Phantom 2-2/0
Thread: Kevlar
Head: Dumbbell eyes, tied Clouser-style
Wing: Synthetic fibres & tinsel in desired colour.

When fishing deep and/or snaggy water for zander, a Clouser-style fly (ie hook point upwards) is often the best choice. Loud, bright colours help to combat murk. In larger sizes this is also a fine pike catcher.

ZANDER BOOBY

Hook: Sakuma Phantom 2-2/0
Thread: Kevlar or other strong thread
Head: Foam tube
Body: Hollow rattle chamber, covered in metallic fritz
Wing: Zonker strip in desired colour
Tail: Section of 'hot' coloured material

Besides heavy flies, booby-style dressings also have potential for bottom-hugging stillwater zander. Like the classic trout flies, these are best presented with a fast sink line and a short leader of just 3-4ft, the buoyancy of the fly keeping it just off the bottom.

NIGHT-WATCHMAN

Hook: Sakuma Manta 2-2/0, with added lead wire
Thread: Black Kevlar
Wing: Mix of Black and Light EP fibres & a pinch of flash material

Side flashes: Luminous strip, combined with grizzle hackle
Head: Epoxy & 3D eyes (Deer Creek)

Whilst night fishing is unnecessary to catch zander, evenings and the first hour or two of darkness can be especially productive and there is an undeniable thrill in the exercise. This fly is designed for just this purpose – a small torch or even a mobile phone can be used to charge the luminescence of the barred strips, which are simply bars of special glow material and grizzle hackle stuck flat with strong adhesive.

Sam Edmonds returns a cracking 13lb Grafham zander.

CHUB

The chub is a fish of contradictions. The big mouth immediately betrays a bold appetite for all manner of prey items, from mayflies to minnows. Indeed, when a good chub engulfs a fly you'll certainly be left in little doubt. But equally this solid, bronze-sided river fish is notoriously wary of human presence. For obvious reasons careless anglers don't catch many chub, which can spook with a single clumsy cast or misplaced footstep. And yet of all the species in these pages, the chub is one of the best of all for fly rod sport.

The subtlety of flyfishing lends itself perfectly to catching chub. Indeed, when fish are visible in clear water you'll find the subtle presentation of the fly angler far less likely to spook chub than that of the fisher using conventional tackle.

This is never truer than in the heat of summer, which is the real prime time for the fly rod. From June onwards, the chub often hold in shallow, well-oxygenated runs. Like trout, you'll find them pointing into the flow, picking off passing morsels. Unlike trout however, chub are a more sociable fish and you only need to spook one before the others also lose interest. A slow, cautious approach is an absolute must, preferably casting upstream so that the chub locates the fly long before it discovers the angler.

CHUB TACKLE & SEASON

TACKLE: Can vary greatly. Although not as strong as trout or carp, chub like snaggy areas and can fight hard. For general fishing with dries and nymphs, a 9-10ft rod and 5-6wt lines will suffice. For smaller rivers with less space and smaller chub, scale down to a shorter 7-8ft 6in rod in 4-5 rating.

Leaders: Typically 12ft or greater in open water or 9ft where space is cramped. Tippets of 4-5lb are suitable. Opt for heavier, 8lb line when using streamers.

Other: Forceps. Waders may be vital on some rivers. If bank fishing, take a generous-sized, long handled net.

SEASON: The coarse season applies on rivers, but in the warmer days from June to September, dry fly sport can be excellent. Heavier nymphs and streamers can extend sport into the autumn and winter.

Stealthily does it

In essence, stealth and careful observation are the crucial factors in chub fishing. Your starting point should be to find a suitable vantage point and simply watch: how many fish are present? Are they holding still in flowing water or roving about? Where might you place your cast to present a fly without spooking the fish? Should I wade or stay on the bank? Might I be better off crossing over and casting from the other side? Get the approach wrong and it's all over in an instant; hence a few moments of careful deliberation can be invaluable. It is always wise to look and look again before you cast because chub are the most unforgiving of all the species in these pages when it comes to the way the angler approaches them.

The better news for the chub angler is that the species is a true opportunist and hence rarely a very fussy eater. If you're stealthy, fly choice can be relatively unimportant and chub will eat just about anything that will fit inside their mouth, from a tiny nymph to a large streamer.

Given a choice, the sheer excitement of presenting a fairly large dry fly is hard to beat. Hoppers, Beetles and even more outlandish dries such as Drone Flies or Daddy Longlegs are all suitable choices, making an excellent mouthful for the greedy chub, who shows a distinct liking for terrestrials.

Where fish are lying deeper,

A solid chub lurks in the shade of a tree. Provided he hasn't spotted the angler, a carefully-aimed fly is liable to be devoured quickly.

however, wet flies such as Czech nymphs and the good old Hare's Ear also work. Streamers, which play on the chub's natural predatory instincts, can also produce fish well however and provide an option for the colder months when the species moves deeper or proves unwilling to rise to an artificial fly.

Trees and Terrestrials

Typical wild chub fishing always makes me think of tight corners and big mouths. My first ever fly-caught chub stands as a typical example: a summer's day, a tangled corner somewhere on a bushy river. The gap beneath two clumps of thick branches looked inviting but would have been scarcely big enough to park a bicycle. Three dark backs swayed gently in the course of the flow; sometimes one of the trio would make a brisk turn and thrust forwards to investigate something moving with the current. A real tackle graveyard, albeit perfect chub habitat.

A Black Hopper, still one of my favourite chub flies, was tied on as I studied this utterly tangled lair, which resembled none of the photographs of pretty swims you see in books or magazines.

I took aim and probably more through luck than judgment, the fly landed just ahead of the first fish. For a second or two the

Living for kicks: Large, leggy terrestrials are excellent fun for chub.

Ben Garnett enjoys a cast on the River Culm, home to many mouthy chub, besides trout.

fly went with the flow, before the chub pushed sideways and upwards and with one gulp of its big mouth, the Hopper vanished from sight.

With a hefty swirl the fish ducked straight under the branches. I managed to keep it from finding any roots, but was left with the sudden realisation that I was in no position to control the chub, let alone net it, crouching as I did on a high bank. The only means to get to the fish was to scramble down and get up to my knees in water. Before either of us had fully come to our senses, I was crashing into the river below, bundling the fish into the net. When the excitement subsided I had a decent chub for a Devon river, my first caught on the fly, at around 2lb.

I've caught better chub since and many from swims just as awkward. Herein lies the battle of chub fishing, especially on the more awkward, bushy rivers.

Steady, open water is one thing but much of what constitutes really classic chub habitat, and the areas they quickly seize a drowning insect, is that of tree cover and snaggy corners.

Getting at Them

Like trout, big chub are wily creatures and can show a preference for the most inaccessible stretches of the water. They really do love those parts of a river which anglers hate! Undercut banks, bends and overhanging bushes are all prime places, if you can only get your fly to the fish rather than simply into the branches.

On larger rivers, some anglers even use boats to combat the problem. For the rest of us, side and roll casts can be invaluable. It is all-too-often a one shot affair. Get it right and the response is immediate and emphatic; misfire and you'll lose the interest of the fish besides your fly. One useful technique to search under trees is to approach from the opposite bank.

Use a long leader and cast directly across into a clear spot, letting the fly carry underneath foliage. You may even have to fly in the face of textbook advice and flip your fly downstream with some slack, in order to let it pass beneath branches for a few brief seconds, but long enough to tempt a hungry chub.

It is just this sort of territory where chub will respond to a meaty terrestrial, dropped as if it had fallen from the trees. In fact, the usual rule of a delicately presented fly need not always be adhered to – beetles, grasshoppers and other bugs certainly don't tend to fall into the drink with any great subtlety and a little plop can quickly pique the interest of a big mouth waiting nearby.

Throwing in the odd twitch to induce takes is also excellent fun with leggy or muddler patterns.

Chub Tackle

There are different approaches to suitable tackle. Naturally, if you are wading in the thick of branches or if casting space from the banks is a problem (which it frequently is) a brook rod of 8ft or so is a handy tool. Where cover or undercut banks lie at close quarters, however, a longer rod (10ft plus) can be used with a minimum of fly line, in a similar manner to the traditional technique of 'dapping' (fishing virtually under the tip of a long rod with a live insect). Indeed, this can be simpler than trying to steer greater lengths of fly line into cramped spaces.

As a kid I remember my father would sometimes use a simple roach pole

A nail-biting scenario. Several nice chub are present, but who spotted who first?

and a mere rod's length of line to literally flick a large, juicy dry fly just beyond the rod tip on the waters of our local stream to take chub.

Chub are not the greatest fighters of the coarse fishes but they do pull hard and fine tackle is an especially lousy idea in snaggy surroundings. Having said this, chub won't tolerate thick line, especially where they encounter anglers regularly. The flex of a light rod can help cushion the fight and protect tippets which are typically 4–5lb breaking strain.

Where branches are a menace, your first step on hooking a chub should be to drop the rod tip low to avoid trailing branches; under the surface if necessary. Like so much in fishing, there is no magic

Chub love to loiter in the very spots anglers hate.
In these confines, a long rod and short line can be useful to 'dap' a juicy artificial.

trick involved in catching chub, but an approach consisting of various careful stages. Convincing the fish to eat your fly is often the smallest part of the challenge: your biggest obstacles are not spooking the fish, getting the fly into an ugly, small space and managing to extract your chub from that same awkward lie.

Streamier Summer Lies

In the heat of summer, chub become more accessible to the river fisher, frequently seeking out those faster and more oxygen-

92

Chub like this 3½ pounder are plentiful and very willing takers on many rivers.

*A warm day on the Wye.
With active chub showing around
cover, Bob James tempted this fish
on a black beetle pattern.*

rich flows in preference to the slacks. So on hot days they can be found in water which many bait fishers might ignore – those streamy runs with a healthy push of shallow water. Indeed, I've sought chub in vain from snaggy holes in warm conditions only to find them in inches of fast water.

Flies & Casting

In such conditions the species behaves more like trout, often sitting nose first into the flow. They feed avidly on prey such as freshwater shrimps and caddis and olive nymphs besides emerging or adult insects.

A large nymph or classic dry fly is an effective way to proceed. I tend to begin with a dry fly, only switching to a nymph if the fish are unwilling to rise. Of course, there are also times when you may not be able to see the fish, in which case a nymph is the answer. In shallow water, the New Zealand dropper method is very effective. In the type of slightly deeper swim which a coarse angler might trot with casters and a stick float, however, a heavy bug such as a Czech nymph is another suitable option, with or without an indicator.

With more space available, casts can be made with less risk. But if only it was so simple as just reaching the fish. Invariably, in faster, more open water both chub and angler become more visible and you simply cannot take enough care to avoid being spotted.

Chub hate any presence on the skyline and are utterly intolerant of clumsy wading. Given a choice, it is best not to wade at all and to keep as low as possible.

There are days the author curses being a six footer, as another chub scatters!

As with trout, flies for steady glides should be presented upstream and allowed to 'dead drift' with the river, so cast well ahead of the fish. Chub can be aggressive, but they don't like a fly dropped right on their nose. Nature is rarely so convenient and these spooky fish are no fools. In clear, open water, tippet strengths can be dropped down to as low as 3lb if required. Longer leaders of 12ft plus are also an advantage where space permits. Not only does this help keep the fly line away from the fish, but allows a few more seconds of drag-free drift on each cast where currents vary. Pure stealth is the key to catching in clear, sunny water. Rivers like the Dorset Stour are a case in point, where the fish gathering in streamy, faster water can be ultra-wary of human presence; and yet sneak up quietly and one tidy cast is all it takes to catch a solid chub. Another notable observation is that even on rivers where the fish become 'educated' having been well-peppered with baits, feeders and floats, the fly still seems to work very well.

The Black Woolly Bugger, my 'go to' streamer pattern for chub.

Battle begins - chub don't fight as hard as trout, but demand balanced tackle capable of soaking up powerful initial lunges.

The Predatory Big-Mouth

A further aspect of chub fishing often overlooked is their predatory nature where larger food items are concerned. Streamers can be an excellent alternative tactic for chub. It wasn't without reason that Izaak Walton and others spoke of the 'catholic' taste of chub, which are well known for taking minnows, sculpins and other small fry.

Streamers and lure style flies are especially useful where sight fishing is tricky or impossible, not to mention when the fish are sheltering in deeper or slightly more coloured water. Specific imitations such as minnows are an enjoyable ruse, but I have caught more chub on the 'general fit' provided by a Woolly Bugger than on all the other streamers in my box put together.

An effective presentation here is to cast upstream and across to swing round in the current. A streamer is always worth a punt presented parallel to undercut banks – the sort of swims which look innocuous but on closer inspection reveal undercuts as deep as your leg. Indeed, the Woolly Bugger takes fish all year round and with some experimentation can be used to extend the chub fisher's year into the cooler months when the fish retreat into deeper water.

Looking at the impressive size of a chub's mouth, I've often wondered about using much bigger flies for the species and this is a line of enquiry I intend to pursue further. Were it not for wire traces, perhaps a good deal more would fall to pike flies on rivers.

The list of larger prey doesn't begin and end with fish either. Many waters

*Wrestled from cover. Relief as a
nice mid-sized fish comes to hand.*

containing crayfish see chub grow quickly on these invaders, as do other coarse species. Scant few have tried matching artificials so far, partly due to a lack of fly patterns. A little borrowing from our American friends, who love to present 'crawfish' for predatory fish, could just be the answer.

What seems certain is that like trout, the really large chub do not reach their hulking size by feeding on spindly little insects. The old adage of 'a big mouthful for a big fish' might be worth taking into account here with some super-sized flies to mimic anything from roach fry to gudgeon and even dace. Call it far-fetched if you like – but chub are known for stealing whole sprats and fairly large plugs from pike anglers, whilst another angling friend once took a chub of over 5lb on a mouse-style surface lure. Don't let the skittish nature of the chub fool you into thinking he is a dainty eater.

Whether chub mistake streamers as food is a matter for debate but even the more outlandish lures work. I personally believe that the species has a mean streak that has more to do with instinctive aggression than hunger. Certainly you can quite often get a quick response from a disinterested-looking fish by presenting a vigorously moving streamer.

The catapult cast is an invaluable technique when back-casting is impossible – a simple case of using the flex of the rod to ping the fly a short distance.

A summer chub from the Stour. This one took in no more than two feet of water.

FOOD FOR THOUGHT: WHAT DO CHUB WANT?

The list of natural items and baits a chub will eat is mind-boggling. So where does the flyfisher begin? Any suitable fly might work, but we can divide our artificials roughly by season.

Summer is a time of plenty. As the temperature rises, you will often find chub just under the surface and willing to rise, often in streamy, well-oxygenated water. Bait anglers catch them on slugs, bread and even elderberries and dapped grasshoppers. For the flyfisher, we'd recommend copying sedges (G&H sedge, Elk Hair Caddis, small Muddlers, Klinkhamers), olives (Beacon Beige, Adams) or any of the terrestrials (Hopper, Stimulator, daddy longlegs, flying ant).

Autumn is usually the time to switch to nymphs. Caddis larvae and year-round staples such as freshwater shrimp are a good bet. Try any of the following: Czech Nymph, Pink Shrimp, Hare's Ear, Peeping Caddis. Fry are also abundant - and chub will eat fingerling coarse fish, including minnows.

Winter - heavy nymphs are still worth trying, but with the fish far less willing to shift from the bottom, be prepared to search deeper. The fish also become more reliant on prey such as fish fry and minnows, so try switching to streamers (Epoxy Minnow, Woolly Bugger, Wiggle Sculpin, Appetizer, Jig Fly).

CHUB FLIES

BLACK WOOLLY BUGGER

Hook: Long Shank Lure, 6-10
Head: Black Tungsten bead
Thread: Black
Tail: Black Marabou
Rib: Silver Wire
Body: Black dubbing
Body Hackle: Palmered black cock

Besides the smaller insects, chub also prey on small fish and much larger nymphs and will readily take a streamer. Providing a good silhouette and plenty of movement, the Black Woolly Bugger is an excellent all-rounder.

HARRY POTTER

Hook: Wet Fly 8-12
Thread: Red
Body: Magic glass or nymph body stretch
Wing: Deer hair & white antron
Legs: Knotted pheasant fibres
Thorax: Black dubbing
Head Hackle: Black hen

I first encountered this fly on Chew reservoir. It has since proved a cracking fly for chub, which simply love hoppers. This one sits low in the water and is ultra-visible, whilst the deer hair makes it a buoyant, tough cookie.

This fine chub fell to a simple deerhair sedge pattern (see Muddler Sedge opposite)

COACHMAN

Hook: Dry fly 10-14
Thread: Dark brown
Body: Peacock
Wings: Goose
Hackle: Red cock

Any number of good-sized traditional dry flies will take chub. The Coachman is just one of them, and although you're likely to lose a few, it has the advantage of being a simple to tie, readily available pattern.

MUDDLER SEDGE

Hook: Long shank dry 8-12
Thread: Brown
Head: Tightly bunched and clipped deer hair
Wing: Deer hair
Body: Coarse dubbing: brown, green or tan

Chub like a juicy sedge fly and patterns which can be waked without sinking are excellent fun, on warm evenings especially. Cast this one close to surface activity and expect smash takes!

CARTY'S GT
(General Terrestrial)

Hook: Wide gape 4-10
Thread: Black
Abdomen: Yarn covered by palmered black cock
Head & overbody: Black Deer hair
Wings: Synthetic winging material
Legs: Rubber strands
Back Sighter: Tuft of red yarn or similar

My brother found this fly in New Zealand. It was intended for trout – but to me just screamed chub! Leggy terrestrials such as this are superb fun flipped as close to cover as you dare.

Wily, strong and great fun on a fly rod, carp are an exciting diversiom for any flyfisher.

CARP

A creature of wily temperament and great power when hooked, carp have rapidly become an obsession for many thousands of anglers. Their appeal is simple and undeniable: carp grow to an impressive size and are a challenging quarry capable of giving the fight of a lifetime on the right tackle. Perhaps the only mystery is why flyfishing for these heavyweights has taken so long to become established.

Like the rainbow trout, the carp is a non-native species that has somehow joined our landscape to become as British as fish and chips or football. No freshwater fish epitomises the transformation of angling in British waters more than the carp, with stillwaters everywhere providing both quantity and quality. Ironically, in the midst of 'carp fever' many trout lakes have been turned into carp fisheries.

All the more reason perhaps that flyfishermen should reclaim some lost territory and experience these rod-bending fish for themselves. But equally, existing carp addicts won't find a more sporting or intimate way to do battle with the species.

CARP TACKLE & SEASON

TACKLE: An 8# set-up is about right for carp. You might get away with a 7wt for 'fun-sized' carp on a day ticket water, but for bigger fish a 9 wouldn't be over the top. Select a powerful, dependable rod for these strong, tenacious fighters.

Leaders: Should be a single length of line or tapered leader of between 6 and 12lb strength, depending on snags and the size of fish present. Avoid the potential weak points of knotted leaders made of different line strengths.

Other: Forceps and a generous-sized landing net. Many fisheries also insist on an unhooking mat. Do check the rules.

SEASON: Carp fishing is available year round, but the best flyfishing tends to coincide with warm periods when the fish grow more active and come up in the water to feed, usually from May to September.

Surface Browsers

A carp lake in high summer: the perfect setting for some delicate presentation to cruising fish.

Undoubtedly the finest time for fly rod carping is during the warmer months of summer, when fish of all sizes bask the surface of lakes for food. Both artificial bait imitations and more natural flies have their place. Whichever you select however, the craftiness of carp is legendary. Careful presentation is essential, for in spite of the big mouth and great appetite, the carp has one of the most picky mouths of any freshwater fish, its rubbery lips and sensitive whiskers (or 'barbules') adept at investigating and rejecting suspicious mouthfuls in an instant.

This natural caginess of the carp can make the finesse of flyfishing especially useful. You can cast to cruising fish more gently than with conventional tackle. It is certainly less intrusive than a splashy weight or float rig and carp don't seem to be unduly alarmed by fly line. With a little practise you can even be selective, picking off the fish of your choice.

Fly rod carping can range from tackling the tamest pond to a wild and overgrown lake. Whilst the latter habitats make for a particularly challenging and fascinating exercise, both little ponds and wild lakes offer exciting flyfishing. But perhaps the most consistent sport as well as the ideal introduction for those finding their feet comes from the tamer surroundings of modern, man-made fisheries.

This browsing double-figure carp took a stimulator, presented in an overgrown swim on a warm evening.

104

SURFACE TRICKS FOR CRAFTY CARP

Since more often than not flyfishing for carp is a dry fly affair for clear, sunny days, our line can be a real giveaway to the fish. Just like a river angler casting for fussy trout, presentation is key. One useful ploy is to degrease your leader with Fullers earth, 'leader sink' or similar, which kills fish-spooking reflection. Other dodges include using smaller or different coloured offerings. A size 10 hook is far less suspicious than a number 4. For obvious reasons, thick leaders are conspicuous and the ideal solution is a single length of a low diameter, high tech line such as Frog Hair, Drennan 'Double Strength' (see picture) or a quality co-polymer. Flexible materials fare better than stiffer, springier brands which carp may sense and reject. As with flies, try to think about the 'feel' of terminal tackle as well as its appearance.

On weedier waters light line can be suicidal however. One useful dodge here is to use existing vegetation such as lilies or duck weed to conceal a thicker leader from suspicious eyes.

Casting in a Small Lake

While carp will investigate various food items, a great deal of modern carp fishing takes place on waters where baits such as bread and dog biscuits are the norm. Purists may sniff, but for the rest of us, suitable imitations made of deer hair, cork or other materials can be presented to great effect on a fly rod. Unlike the bait angler, these have the advantage that they won't come off the hook and we can dispense with floats and other gadgets to enable a simple, stealthy presentation.

A quick word is perhaps necessary on etiquette here. Most fishery owners

The ideal set-up for stalking carp in a man-made lake: dog biscuits, catapult, a tough little flyrod and a reel with plenty of backing.

A classic English carp pond. Quiet, more overgrown pools are the places to try the 'natural' approach (see page 109).

have no problem with flyfishing, provided sensible tackle is used. Such waters can be busy though and it should go without saying that consideration and space should be given to others. Always keep checking behind you when you cast. You may even receive some odd looks – but the vast majority of anglers will simply be peaceful onlookers, friendly and curious if you stop and chat.

Casting space is not always abundant at man-made lakes either and where hazards and other bank users are nearby the fly angler's objective should be to travel light, seeking out quieter areas with visible fish and a little room to manoeuvre. Don't despair if you only manage a short roll cast though: carp will come in very close if you are stealthy.

Coaxing Carp to Feed

Spotting the fish and finding a likely area is often simple enough: convincing these cruising carp to take a fly is another matter. The key factor is the task of coaxing the fish to feed and this involves a skill more familiar to the coarse angler, that of loose feeding. A supply of bait and a catapult are essential in this exercise in gauging the response of the fish and encouraging the carp to let their mouths rule their heads. The classic rule of 'little and often' is usually the best way to proceed: use too little bait and the carp will remain picky or lose interest; put in too much and the fish will have too much choice.

Your aim is to get the carp gobbling up free offerings confidently, expecting to find fresh bait on a regular basis. It is often worth resisting the urge to cast. Simply feed the fish for half an hour or more to get the desired effect and really let a few hungry mouths settle.

Carp Takes

The takes themselves can be a sticking point. The antics of these big-mouthed creatures is a far cry from the sometimes rapid takes of other species and a fast strike is liable to pull the bait out of the carp's mouth or worse still, break the leader. The best advice here is to let the fish take properly. Watch the fly but only strike as you see the last foot or two of line pull tight. A measured lift of the rod is more than adequate to set the hook – use too much force and the weight of the carp will spell certain doom.

Patience Required

It can be a frustrating game, especially if the carp are wary of anglers, but careful presentation and a degree of patience will stack the odds in favour of the fly rod. Unlike with trout, it is unwise to keep casting a dry fly to moving carp. Far better

Critical mass – a basking summer carp. But is this one merely sunbathing, or might he be in the mood for a snack?

Commercial success: a solid mirror carp in man-made surroundings. This one took a deer hair mixer.

In position for carp. Patience can be a virtue with this species, which don't like being 'chased' around the swim with a fly.

to leave the fly for a few minutes at a time in a likely area on the edge of a feeding group of fish. Always try to cast short first and avoid 'chasing' the fish; landing the fly line over the top of the carp too often will only spook them or push the shoal beyond comfortable casting range. The golden rules are: watch and wait; keep adding some free bait in a consistent area rather than peppering the water with casts.

Whichever size carp your chosen lake holds, the curve in a fly rod tells its own story. These are strong fish that will quickly find any weakness in your tackle so do test your knots and be sure that your fly line can follow the fish unobstructed.

It's also a good idea to set your drag quite lightly to give line freely when required. Both rod and nerves may be tested with a good specimen; traditional flyfishing it isn't, but few fish will bend a fly rod quite like the carp.

A More Natural Angle...

Weaning carp onto artificial bait imitations is one aspect of carp flyfishing, but what of wilder, more traditional angling? Those weedier and more classic-looking carp pools are a rewarding option for those who seek more imitative and natural fishing. On such wilder ponds and lakes the fish will be well-accustomed to feeding on snails, nymphs and all manner of other prey items. Suddenly the fly angler has plenty to copy besides bread and a far more exciting challenge altogether awaits.

Carp Food

The range of things that carp will eat is legendary. Bloodworms feature heavily, but in terms of realistic patterns or indeed

Summer highs – a sunny pond and a serious bend in the fly rod.

sight fishing opportunities, I remain to be convinced, never having had much success.

The next phase of the bloodworm's life, the buzzer, is of course another staple of waters both wild and tame but whilst I have taken occasional carp on buzzers and small emergers, many lakes contain too many stunted roach and other greedy smaller fish to make this a viable option. Hence most of my natural flies for carp in mixed waters tend to be larger, meatier mouthfuls.

The water itself should provide those important clues in fly selection, but carp can and will accept various food items and the field is wide open here.

Wind and heavy rain can wash unfortunate creatures into the water and onto the menu: slugs are one casualty of floods, whilst in different conditions beetles, moths and other terrestrials also end up in the drink.

On lakes with plenty of vegetation, carp are likely to find plenty of little bonuses through the summer and if I'm honest I always pity those waters where the trees are cut back or even removed.

A beetle or other large dry may not be as efficient as a 'bait' fly then, but a suitable-looking creepy crawly placed in the path of a browsing carp may well be intercepted. Such captures may sound unusual but are nothing new and in fact savvy carp anglers have already enjoyed success tricking carp on pieces of black foam fashioned with strands to simulate legs. Nobody declares these captures as 'eccentric'.

Carp can be every bit as wary as surface-feeding trout and part of the knack is in watching cruising fish carefully. Try to anticipate and land the fly a few feet in advance of moving fish, rather than drop an artificial on the carp's nose.

More often than not the accidental discoveries provided by nature appear as odds and ends rather than a 'hatch'. In the absence of one distinct food item then, any suitable dry fly is worth a trial, although a quick recce of the waterside may yield a few clues.

Falling Caterpillars

Just occasionally the fly angler can capitalise on a surprising abundance of one food source. One particular example of such natural opportunism which stands out in my mind occurred on a tree-lined pool of perhaps just an acre.

One summer there were regular disturbances where two old trees reached over the water. For a while I couldn't fathom what was happening; the carp certainly didn't seem very keen on bread. As I stood next to the overhanging branches, the mystery was solved with an audible 'plop' as a light green caterpillar hit the water. Within seconds a giant pair of lips broke the surface, casually sucking it in. A quick study of the lower branches revealed many more of the caterpillars. It was perhaps no surprise that bread was off the menu and I remain convinced that a suitable caterpillar imitation could have yielded some spectacular results.

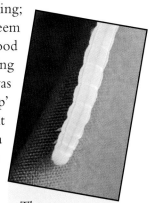

The light green caterpillar was clearly the preferred item on the menu that day.

Sipping the Snails

Whilst such events don't represent everyday occurrences, other prey items are far more dependable. The humble freshwater snail, for example, is a true staple present in vast quantities on just about any weedy water. The mysterious sucking sounds amongst lily pads so characteristic of summer carp ponds is often the sound of snails being plundered. The sticky egg clusters of the snail are greedily devoured, but with powerful throat teeth, carp are also partial to the fully-grown adults which also inhabit the weeds.

A good deal of these can be found in or near the surface film in warm weather and a simple snail fly presented close by can be an excellent choice.

Failing this, tantalising trout flies such as the Black and Peacock can also tempt these snail diners. Be warned, however: these weed-hugging carp may need strong leaders and decisive action to wrestle them from their sanctuary.

Numerous other alternatives are open to the adventurous fly angler catering for the carp and its wide ranging, unpredictable tastes which include every-thing from tadpoles and fish fry through to nymphs and the eggs of other fish. More commonly, heavy hatches of sedge or buzzers can switch the fish onto these creatures, often much to the frustration of biteless carp anglers using conventional tactics.

Wet Flies

Whilst I have enjoyed some degree of success with wet flies fished static or simply allowed to hang in the water, plenty of captures have been recorded on somewhat larger nymphs retrieved slowly for carp to pursue, and certainly flies such as living nymphs and natural looking Damsels

The Cork Mixer, a brilliant fly to use when the carp are feeding keenly on dog biscuits.

A carp has only one way to find out if something is edible and that's to chomp it! Be warned though, carp have sensitive mouths and will blow out suspicious or inedible objects as quickly as they take them in.

Who says flyfishing is fanciful stuff?
Andy Parkinson took this stunning brace
of twenty pounders on a fly rod on a lake
more commonly tackled with bite alarms
and boilies.

pique their interest. The fish will follow or turn to look, but more often than not I have struggled to convince them to take the fly, the occasional bite only occurring from a fly sneaked in very slowly or better still tweaked along and then just left to hang in the water as a fish shows interest. Quite often carp like to cruise in the upper layers but won't take a dry fly and it's in these circumstances that a natural, slow sinking fly may be intercepted.

There is no doubt that the typical waters available play a huge part in flyfishing for carp in the UK.

In America these fish were seldom cast for, regarded as 'trash fish' even. The Yanks are quickly changing their tune though and catch carp on all sorts of flies, even lures such as the Woolly Bugger. On our shores though, they are often subjected to intense fishing pressure, a good reason in itself to try the very different approach

of flyfishing perhaps, but our fisheries are also commonly murky, limiting flyfishing to the upper layers of the water.

Take it from Me

For the record, I have seldom ever found fishing 'blind' for carp worthwhile. Populations do go undetected in the corners of some of our wilder lakes and reservoirs though, and in these clear, less disturbed environments there is far greater scope for experimentation with natural fly patterns.

In many ways, carp and their habitats vary as much as those of trout. River fishing is another area where the field is wide open: the corners of weir pools can

Top: Carp waters vary immensely. Besides the many commercial lakes peppered with artificial baits, the species also thrives in some beautiful secluded locations.

Above: This small common intercepted a bloodworm presented close to the bottom, in clear, shallow water.

Andy Parkinson took this stunning common carp in the sort of bushy swim most anglers avoid. A roll cast put his fly right in the path of the fish.

hold browsing carp in the summer, which will happily pick through debris and look for any food items washed into view. Experiments continue with this fascinating species, which has a wider-ranging appetite than many anglers imagine.

I can only hope my own notes here will assist the intrepid carp fisher. But in truth, unlike the mass of information on conventional carp tactics, much of the flyfishing rulebook has yet to be written. Perhaps this is what makes the flyfishing approach to the wily, muscular carp so fascinating.

MOODY CARP

Carp can be wily, temperamental creatures, but it helps to establish the 'mood' of the fish. Carp busily sucking around lilies and weedy cover are worth covering with a floating pattern such as a snail (see below left). Another phenomenon is that of carp which cruise the upper layers but refuse dry flies. These tricky customers will sometimes take a slow sinker, such as a Black and Peacock, or buzzer, as it falls. A fish which stoops periodically on the bottom, almost standing on its head, is definitely browsing the bottom for food; so perhaps a static or very gently twitched fly might work? Other fish you spot moving more hurriedly are simply 'travellers' and are nigh-on uncatchable.

PLAYING CARP

Hooking your carp can often be only one half of the challenge of netting a fish. Big fish and snags can make this a hairy business. So how do you halt a weighty carp (or any large fish for that matter!) on the rampage? The old cliché of keeping the rod up is not always a great help here.

In practise a low rod angle *(see below)* is preferable in situations where you need to exert maximum stopping power and it also tires fish quicker. Other hazards such as overhanging trees and obstacles may call for a quick reaction. With trailing branches, for example, the rod tip can be sunk under the water. Above all, use adequate tackle and have courage. You'll find it hard to break off on a balanced set-up with 8lb plus line. And remember, that fly rod is meant to bend!

MIXING IT UP

Carp love floating baits, but can be frustratingly good at avoiding the artificial version. One trick with deer hair copies is to give the fly a good dunking before use. This helps it to sit low in the water like the real thing. Regular, accurate feeding is often the real knack however. One trick I learned from match angler Steve Lockett is to flick out baits literally non-stop – just one or two biscuits each time. By throwing or catapulting these high so that they "pop" down onto the water, the carp quickly learn to home in. If you can get a group of fish competing, so much the better.

WINNING THE MARGINS WITH THE FLOATING BREAD FLY!

On so many man-made fisheries, the one area consistently neglected is the margin. Carp quickly get used to finishing off bread and baits that end up close to, or even underneath, the bank. If there is a breeze, this will often occur on the side of the lake the wind blows into. Listen out for tell-tale slurps at the edge.

My favourite offering for winkling out these fish is the bread imitation *(see picture)*, often little more than lowered into the right area, close to hungry mouths. Allow a split second for the artificial to disappear, and then lift into the fish – a hard strike at such close quarters and you might break the tippet in an instant. This can be exciting, close-contact sport for the opportunist.

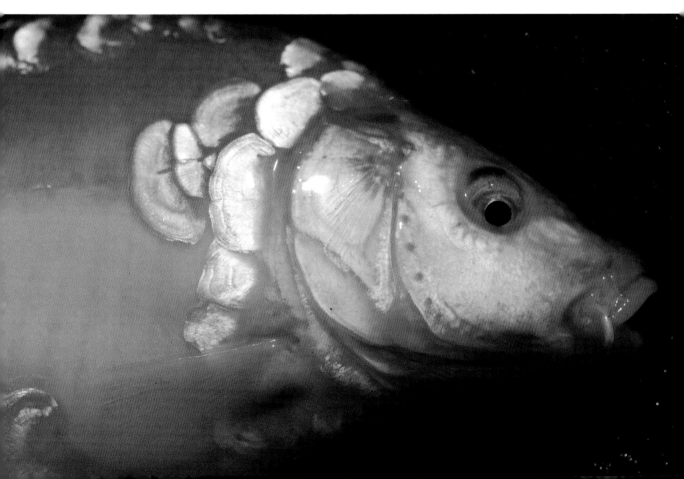

CARP FLIES

BONIO

Hook: Barbless,
extra strong dry
fly 4-10
Thread: Tan
Body: Clipped
deer hair
Sight tuft:
Orange yarn

Deer hair flies represent a basic, enduring
way to catch carp feeding on mixers.
These are now readily available to buy,
although the home tyer can create sizes
and colours to their own preferences; a
little, bright sight tuft helps the fly stand
out from your loose feed.

CORK MIXER (see page 112)

Hook: Barbless
carp 4-10
Body: Cork – real
or synthetic

It doesn't get much
simpler than this.
When a deer hair
fly proves too easy to reject, this can be
the answer and you can even carefully
insert some weight into the cork to make
it sit lower in the surface film. My own
preference is for the slightly spongy,
synthetic cork. And it's a good excuse to
drink more wine.

BREAD FLY

Hook: Barbless carp
2-10
Thread: White
Underside: White
marabou fibres
Top: Folded white
foam

Carp will take bread just about
anywhere. I like a fly with some softness
as well as toughness and buoyancy, and
marabou adds this feel to my bread
pattern. Sinking patterns are also easily
fashioned from a simple pinch of white
marabou on a hook.

CATERPILLAR

Hook: Long shank
dry or sedge 6-12
Thread/Head:
Black
Body: Green poly
yarn or foam
Legs/Hair:
Palmered grizzle hackle

Carp are curious feeders that will take a
vast range of food at the surface. Caterpillars are irresistible fun to try – smaller
grubs can also be made without the legs
to replicate less hairy beasts.

STIMULATOR

Hook: Long shank dry 6-12
Thread: To match body
Tail & wing: Deer hair
Body: Dubbed seals fur or synthetic yarn
Body Hackle: Palmered furnace cock
Rib: Fine gold wire
Head: Grizzle cock over orange dubbing

This loud, bushy American dry fly offers a juicy mouthful that might represent a whole plethora of food items: a big sedge, a struggling moth, even a hopper.

FLOATING SNAIL

Hook: Carp 8-12
Shell: Rolled black foam, glued & varnished
Inner: Spectra-blend dubbing (light hare's ear)/ partridge

Snails are an especially common snack for carp on weedy waters – listen out for the sucking sounds as carp slurp at both adults and egg clusters. This fly is created by carefully rolling and gluing a strip of black, fly tyers' foam. For a slow sinking pattern, consider also the classic Black and Peacock (see 'Really Useful Fly Patterns' section).

YELLOW EGG FLY

Hook: Forged wide gape, size 10
Thread: Yellow
Body: Bright yellow egg fly yarn

A yellow egg fly makes a nice obvious target for passing carp. Typically, this would be fished on the bottom – but with regular loose-fed corn, an egg fly can also be fished on the drop. A little weight, such as lead wire or tungsten putty, can be used to alter the sink rate of the fly.

LIVING LEACH

Hook: Keel Hook size 6-10
Thread: Black
Tail: Black marabou
Body: Turns of flexifloss over thread, well varnished

If you can find a carp water with good water clarity and low pressure, they can be persuaded to go for larger living nymph-style patterns – or why not a leech? This fly uses a keel hook to fish 'point up' close to the bottom. For nymphing on the deck, try a painfully slow retrieve.

This rudd was one of several nice fish browsing beneath tree cover. It took a spider pattern within seconds of touching down.

RUDD

In many ways rudd are the perfect diversion for a flyfisher. These beautiful, golden-scaled fish are easily located, take a fly well and offer delightful sport on light tackle. One look at the mouth and its protruding lower lip quickly tells you this is a creature designed to look up for its food, picking off flies and other morsels at the surface.

Rudd fishing is epitomised by summer afternoons on weedy waters, armed with just a handful of flies and a healthy dose of wanderlust. Furthermore, the handsome rudd is an obliging species even in those hot conditions so poor for trout. Another bonus is that a typical day's fishing is often to be had for little more than the price of a pint of beer.

The places rudd are found are perhaps one factor causing their neglect, for despite their presence in many modern commercial fisheries the really prime rudd habitat tends to be overgrown lakes, canals and drains.

It is lamentable that so many fishing clubs and fisheries seem obsessed with hacking back any form of vegetation, thus removing a great deal of insect life – food for fish such as rudd in plain terms. Unspoiled, weedy and rich waters tend to be the best rudd fisheries of all. Such quiet places are seldom convenience fishing

RUDD TACKLE & SEASON

TACKLE: Although a cute 7-8ft trout wand in the 1-4wt class makes a delightful tool for rudd where space allows, longer rods tend to be a good deal more practical for the wilder waters and overgrown banks where quality rudd fishing is found. A 9 or better still a 10ft blank in the 3-5wt class with a floating line is ideal – the sort of set-up you might use for light Czech nymphing.

Leaders & Tippets: These should be as long as is practical. 10-12ft is a good starting point. Tippets should be relatively fine – perhaps as light as 2lb strength for shy fish in clear conditions.

Other: A long handled landing net is a must where banks are awkward. Fine forceps or a disgorger.

SEASON: June to September is prime time, with sunny weather best for dry fly sport. On waters with no close season, such as some lakes and canals, spring can also be productive.

and sometimes the successful rudd angler must be prepared to walk long distances and make the most of tight or overgrown swims. Locations such as clear canals and drains, from rural Somerset to the Fens, are all known for their fine rudd; the lochs of Ireland are another classic destination. Any weedy, forgotten water may have good rudd fishing, with former trout ponds, brick pits and other neglected places all worthy of investigation.

Commercial fisheries are another enjoyable option. Indeed many anglers will appreciate the better casting space, but the rudd tend to be rather smaller in size and lacking the beautiful coloration and condition of the truly wild, clear water fish.

The one often vital criteria with rudd, as with much flyfishing, is that we can see the fish or at least the rise forms they produce. The summer months when fish browse freely in the upper water layers are ideal for rudd fishing, although sunny autumn days can also offer excellent sport. Evening is perhaps the best time of all to be on the water, when flies are abundant and the temperature cools.

Polaroids Essential

It is seldom difficult to locate rudd with a pair of polarising glasses; shoals of smaller fish can be vast, while the larger fish are found in smaller groups. Large rudd, of over 1lb, are found in sparser pods of fish, sometimes made up of just two to three fish and you'll frequently find these elders of the tribe cruising in separate groups or on the fringes of their massed smaller relatives.

A stroll with polarising glasses may quickly reveal the size and numbers of rudd present. The issue is not so much spotting the fish, therefore, but the danger of the fish spotting you. Boat fishermen have long noted their dislike of anything other than a subtle approach. For the bank

The moment of truth: a large rudd homes in on an emerger. If your nerves can stand it, give the bigger fish a split second longer before striking.

Action! Rudd won't give you arm-ache – but light tippets and the overgrown places they love, demand careful, steady playing.

fisher, making use of any available cover is a useful strategy. A light breeze can be a mercy and you should try to move slowly and deliberately into position.

Gently Does It

A minimum of casting strokes should be used if at all possible. Many of us make more false casts than we need; cutting back to just one or two back casts is good practise here and our aim is a tidy, subtle delivery. Indeed, wave a fly rod vigorously or stand too tall against the skyline and you will soon witness the telltale signs of spooky rudd.

It's always worth paying attention to your shadow and the angle of the sun. The species are used to looking up for signs of danger as well as food, and alarmed shoal mates will quickly start to flash and warn one another. Needless to say, skittish rudd are unlikely to take a fly. Hooking a fish will also have a similar effect in clear water and quite often nearby rudd will need time to settle again after you've caught a fish. Another good reason to keep on the move.

Stalking the Surface

While rudd will happily take nymphs and wet flies, perhaps the real cream of rudd sport is on dry flies. The species is an avid surface feeder and on warm, settled days and evenings you can often see the surface of a suitable water dotted everywhere with rise forms. Any smallish, dark fly may be

Devon fly angler Ian Nadin looks understandably delighted with this beautifully chunky canal rudd. It took a Black & Peacock Spider.

taken and a dapper presentation is far more important than any specific fly pattern. In the course of many happy afternoons stalking the species I have caught rudd on flies ranging from a size 22 black gnat to a size 10 hopper.

Food & Flies

The natural diet of rudd is fairly varied and the size of artificial can be important. In high summer you may find the rudd splashing at insects blown onto the water from the undergrowth. Just as often, rudd will browse the surface film for tiny food items including very small insects and fragments of weed. Buzzers are another staple but larger, fast sinking artificials are often quickly shunned and a light, sparsely

dressed fly in size 16 or smaller may be required to pick out the fish. I always keep a selection of tiny flies right down to size 20s in case the fish are refusing the usual fare. Spotting these patterns can be a nightmare – one dodge is to include at least a hint of colour that will contrast against the weed or a dark bottom, with a white CDC a useful material.

Given a choice – and some sunshine – my usual course of action is to start with floating patterns and keep moving until I spot rudd, or at least the rise forms. The hotter the weather gets and the higher the temperature, the more active the rudd become. In the cool of the spring you might need tiny Spiders and Buzzers to tempt shy fish but by June don't be too surprised to watch the fish seize a size 12 Black and Peacock with a response bordering on aggression.

When the fish are active, you can get an excited response from nearby fish by kissing the surface with the fly a few times before you make your final delivery;

ADAPTABLE EMERGERS

If you are unsure whether a dry or wet fly may be best for rudd, an emerger is an excellent option. By presenting a fly that sits 'in' rather than 'on' the surface you have a very adaptable pattern. If the rudd rise to take it, all well and good. But if not, simply give the line a quick tweak and you have a slow sinking fly to cater for those rudd unwilling to come up to the surface.

just watch the rudd dash in eagerly.

As with trout, a slow sinking or dry fly often meets with an instant response and I find it better to cast to moving fish than to leave the fly static for longer periods. A fly cast too close can spook your quarry, but land it gently just 2-3ft in front as if a natural had just touched down on the surface and your rudd will often take without hesitation. If you are stealthy enough, a long rod can be used to 'dap' for rudd, literally dropping the fly just off the rod tip with virtually no fly line required.

Hitting rudd bites is a matter of timing. Although the small fish can be lightning fast and need an instant strike, it is usually better to wait for a split second longer before striking if a really decent one takes the fly. Big rudd will take a fly in a less snatchy manner which is worth remembering when you see a good-sized gold flank home in on your artificial. An instant too long however and rudd can quickly spit out the offending object. Welcome to the fun and frustration of rudd fishing!

Of course, there may be plenty of times when you cannot clearly see a wet fly, in which case you must rely partly on instinct. As soon as you spot a rudd rush forward or tilt upwards and the lips gobble, it's a pretty safe bet your fly has been taken. If in doubt, strike! Sometimes

One on the CDC buzzer. A smallish, slow sinking wet fly is perhaps the deadliest tactic of all for rudd.

It pays to use slow-sinking flies for rudd. If you can get the fly in a position where the fish must rise slightly to take a nymph, this is far superior to a fly dropping past them.

you need a bit of luck with the blurring opening and closing motion of the rudd's lips on the take: strike as they flash open and you're simply left with a confused rudd as the fly pops out.

More on Wet Flies…

There are days in the fisherman's year when rudd refuse to rise to the surface and a nymph or wet fly is the answer. On some occasions, the rudd simply take the wets more willingly and a whole host of flies fit the bill here. Certain considerations must be met however and a fairly common denominator is to keep the fly relatively small. Rudd do not have the biggest mouths and you will hook more rudd on a pattern that can be neatly engulfed. Usual sizes are from 14-18, although a

On overgrown waters such as the Somerset Levels, a long rod is a massive advantage.

rudd of ½lb plus will manage a size 10 just fine and on productive waters, such an offering may prove far more rewarding since the little rudd can't manage it.

A fly that can be seen is also an advantage and the only indication you may receive of a take could be the disappearance of the fly. I have only had scant success with some of the more obvious traditional patterns however – Goldheads seem to get a wary response, the flash perhaps appealing more to predators such as chub and trout. Equally, I believe it wise to include plenty of drab and dark patterns in the fly box if the water is very clear – a little colour is better than a lot, and rudd don't like overkill with trigger points.

You may also find that these sub-surface rudd need a few seconds to find and accept the fly. For this reason, weighted patterns that quickly sink out of sight can be ineffective and I much prefer a nymph which sinks only very slowly or even hangs in the water, affording maximum time for the fly to remain visible to both rudd and angler. The fly tyer can benefit by using lighter gauge hooks and materials such as herl and CDC to create patterns with a suitably slow descent.

Rudd which are taking nymphs can be even more lightning-fast than those sipping dry flies. Sometimes several fish in a row will flatly ignore a wet fly, whilst feeding fish can also rapidly reject an artificial. As with roach, where sight fishing is difficult or impossible, a team of nymphs fished either by touch or beneath a small indicator can be a reasonable alternative tactic, (see the notes in the roach chapter

Access is so often the issue when tackling rudd. A boat can be invaluable on lakes, but your approach should be cautious.

for more on this) although I shudder to think how many bites go completely undetected. As with sight fishing, for the rudd angler there is only one solution to fast bites and fish which can quickly spit out the fly: strike promptly when the chance arises.

Golden Wonders

Rudd fishing with a fly rod is terrific and highly visual fun, but wherever carried out, it is best pursued with a minimum of tackle and a willingness to rove the banks and experiment. Some days a tiny dry fly will work wonders, whilst on others a fairly large nymph can be met with surprising vigour. It can be a frustrating game at times, but for every take missed or fish spooked there is always another shoal of rudd further along the bank.

Although small fish are numerous, catching a big, wily rudd is always an achievement – but a distinct possibility if you can locate one or two. They are often quite patchy in their appearance and won't come to you so the key is to walk and search for them. The beauty of flyfishing for rudd is that it can be discriminating – unlike bait fishing when every fish in the shoal, from the very smallest, wants to take the maggots.

Below: Mobility is essential in tracking down larger rudd, which often seem to be long-term residents in undisturbed areas.

Inset: My 'rudd bugs' are soft-hackled wet flies, with CDC fragments in the dubbing help them to hang temptingly in the upper layers where the rudd like to feed.

Big Rudd

The better rudd tend to crop up in the really prime areas. In those places where food and cover are plentiful, you might just find some of these old survivors in their own small groups and with a careful, accurate cast you can pick these out. As mentioned, the biggest rudd are easier to strike than their quicksilver little brothers and sisters, having bigger mouths and a slower, more ponderous manner of sucking in a fly. Your own approach should be equally unhurried: move slowly, watch closely and present your fly deftly. You might be surprised at just how willingly one of these brilliant gold-sided fish will take a fly.

Above all, the rudd is a fish to be enjoyed. Their habit of mouthing and spitting the fly may make you curse but their sheer beauty will brighten any day's fishing and provide many a happy adventure where that 'quick cast or two' develops into several engaging hours of fun.

A brace of rudd for over three pounds, taken just under the surface from an overgrown swim.

RUDD FLIES

PARACHUTE EMERGER

Hook: Size 12-20 Emerger
Thread: Brown or black 8/0
Post: 2-3 CDC plumes
Body: Seals fur or sub
Rib: Fine flat tinsel or mylar
Thorax: Peacock herl
Hackle: Grizzle cock, tied parachute-style

A terrific all-rounder, this fly is easily spotted by both rudd and angler alike. Scale down a little if the fish are fussy or you're struggling to hook fish – sometimes an overly large parachute hackle can make a fly hard to suck in properly. Equally, a soft CDC post makes a more easily engulfed fly than stiffer materials.

MINI HOPPER:

Hook: Size 12-16 Dry
Thread: Black 8/0
Tag (optional): Bright yarn
Body: Seals fur or sub.
Rib: Fine tinsel or mylar
Legs: Knotted pheasant tail
Hackle: Black cock

If you can stand the fiddle of scaling down the classic hopper patterns, you'll find this leggy little number makes a fine fly. Definitely one to pick out a bigger rudd at the surface.

CRUNCHER

Hook: Size 12-18 nymph style
Thread: Brown or black
Body & tail: Pheasant tail fibres
Rib: Copper wire
Thorax: Peacock herl
Hackle: Furnace hen

The Cruncher is an excellent choice for rudd, a good 'general' pattern which sinks slower than buzzers and other skinny nymphs due to its hackle. The peacock thorax can also be substituted for a 'hot spot' – bright yarn or a tiny pinch of white CDC are both excellent for variants.

RUDD BUG

Hook: Size 12-18 Nymph/Emerger
Thread: Brown 8/0
Body: Mix of hare's ear or spectrablend dubbing and CDC fragments.
Thorax: A tiny pinch of orange or lime ice dubbing.
Rib: Ultra-fine pearl mylar
Hackle: Woodcock or hen

With the use of CDC fibres in a fairly loose dubbing mix, this fly sinks painfully slowly – perfect for rudd, which prefer to come up for their food even when you are offering a wet fly. Light colours show up well against weed, but also try darker variants if the water is clear.

BIBIO

Hook: Size 12-16 Wet fly
Thread: Black
Body: Black & red dubbing
Body hackle: Palmered black hen or cock
Rib: Silver wire

Many of the good old fashioned loch patterns work for rudd. Like other bushy types, the Bibio sinks nice and slowly, shows up well and is especially good in breezy conditions. Avoid excessively long hackles, which the rudd may struggle to suck in. Another useful tip is to sub the cock hackle for softer black hen.

MICRO HERL BUZZER

Hook: Size 14-20 Nymph/Emerger
Thread: Fine brown, olive or black
Body: Stripped quill, biot or pheasant
Rib: Fine copper wire
Head: A few strands of white yarn/ CDC
Thorax: Peacock herl or dubbing

Forget large, heavy-weight buzzers for rudd. Scale down to find the size fish will accept and try a light pattern fished in the surface layers which will sink painfully slowly or suspend (for step-by-step instructions to tie this fly, see pages 210–211).

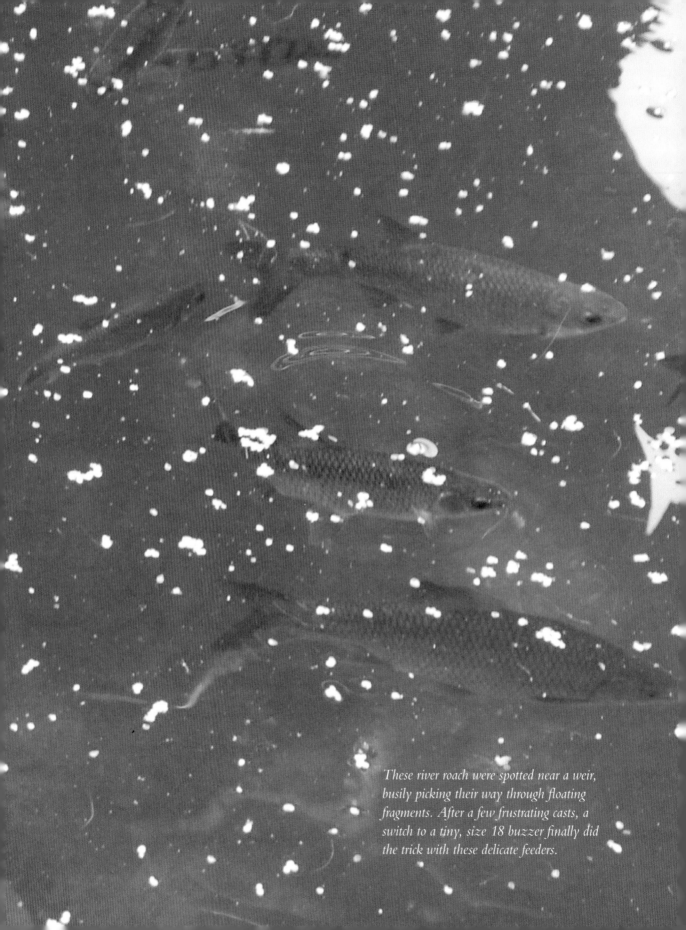

These river roach were spotted near a weir, busily picking their way through floating fragments. After a few frustrating casts, a switch to a tiny, size 18 buzzer finally did the trick with these delicate feeders.

ROACH

The silver flanked, red-finned roach is one of our most widespread fish. With a multitude of habitats and a wide-ranging diet, it is a species to add welcome variety to the flyfishing year.

The species' great adaptability explains a wide distribution and roach can be found everywhere from the chalk streams such as the Test to small farm ponds, feeding on everything from blood-worm to adult midges, snails to silkweed.

Occasional specimens are landed by trout anglers, including 2lb plus reservoir fish, and it is perhaps surprising how seldom such happy 'accidents' occur; until you observe these fish in clear water. Watch roach at close quarters and you will discover just how shy biting these creatures can be. Sure enough, they will take a fly, but often spit it out just as rapidly. Rarely will they move off with a pattern and cause the fly line to move off as trout will, so indications of a take can vary from minor to non-existent.

Tactics

For obvious reasons therefore, it is a major advantage if you can see the fish when it comes to the shy biting roach. A small, buggy nymph is ideal on shallow lakes or canals.

If you still struggle to spot takes, aim for a fly that contrasts suitably: a light-coloured fly can work against dark weeds, a black fly could be better against a light background and you can use the fly's disappearance as your cue to strike.

ROACH TACKLE & SEASON

TACKLE: A light trout set-up is the most enjoyable, sensitive way to pursue the roach. Short brook rods of 1-4 weight can sometimes be used, but where banks are more overgrown a longer blank of up to 10ft is more practical.

Leaders: From 9-12ft. Tippets should be light: 2-3lb co-polymer for dry fly work, or 3-4lb for wets.

Other: A long handled landing net, fine forceps or a disgorger.

SEASON: Summer offers the best chance of dry fly sport, but roach can be taken on wet flies year round.

Many man-made fisheries hold roach and can offer year-round sport – although mild weather and basking fish offer the best action.

On sunny days, or conditions when naturals are hatching, the fish can sometimes be found feeding at the surface but most roach fishing is done with wet flies.

Feeding Roach

The species exhibits a wide diet, as broad in fact as the variety of waters in which this adaptable fish is found. Indeed, the renowned roach expert Dr Mark Everard describes the species as a 'supreme generalist' in his *Complete Book of the Roach*, adding that 'Their diet is limited simply by what they can catch or find, and then

swallow'. River fish, for example, will undoubtedly feed on freshwater shrimp and hence small gammarus look-alikes, such as a tiny Hare's Ear, can work well. Just about any other small prey item you care to name can form staple roach food, from small pond snails right through to occasional predation on fry.

Another notable trend is that roach are heavy feeders of molluscs (water snails, smaller types of freshwater mussels etc) and Everard notes that in some waters these groups represent 'as much as 90%' of the roach's diet. Certainly where weedy, small waters are concerned that excellent pattern for snail feeders, the Black and Peacock Spider, is very effective in smallish sizes.

For both stillwater and river fish there is a favourable overlap with the diet

It is interesting to note that, far from being a 'new' or unusual method, flyfishing for roach has a forgotten history within the sport. Richard Walker was a particularly keen exponent, catching fish from classic English rivers to far-flung lochs. In his estimation, *'the roach fisher who has not learned to use a fly rod is handicapped. He will miss many opportunities... as well as the very deep pleasure that the use of a fly rod affords.'* He took roach to dry flies such as the Black Gnat and even Large Sedges, but rated wet fly fishing more highly, with small flies such as the Pheasant Tail nymph. He notes: *'Sixteen is the most useful size, though sometimes a size 14 is taken readily.... The secret is to let (the fly) sink as far as conditions demand, then to retrieve it slowly and steadily without any jerks, being prepared to strike instantly if the slightest pluck or check is felt.'*

of trout, with buzzers a staple, although for reasons suspected, few roach seem to be caught by accident by trout anglers.

Part of the reason for this could be the average size of artificials used however. Study the mouth of a roach compared with a trout and the difference is glaring. Indeed, of the many common patterns that work for both species (various Buzzers, Daiwl Bach, spiders), I'm inclined to believe that if you're struggling to catch, flies a size or two smaller (generally 14-16) are better for roach, and more likely to be taken decisively into a small, sensitive mouth.

Having said this, a ½lb roach has little trouble accepting a size 10 fly and so your choice may also be shaped by the average size in your water. A 'selective' slightly larger fly may well be worth persevering with if you're after that plump king of the shoal!

On matters of size it is also noticeable how the seasons affect fishing: in warmer times the fish perhaps expect more and bigger insects whereas on cold days I have sometimes only had a response by dropping down to tiny flies.

From experiments in clear water I also suspect a buggy, loose dubbed fly or a soft hackle such as a Spider is more likely to be held onto for that split second longer. Flies like Buzzers and the excel-lent Daiwl Bach do work, but could roach feel the hook quicker with harder-bodied or underdressed patterns?

The Laid-Back Approach

Another important point with roach is to take into account their less than aggressive nature. Whilst trout respond to flies which are twitched or agitated, you should let your nymphs simply hang in the water for roach. The fish may turn towards the fly as it is tweaked into position, but usually the best course of action is then just to let the fish take the fly with minimal interference. Flies which suspend or are dressed to sink painfully slowly are useful, to allow your roach time to respond. Much of the advice on rudd applies here. Refusals are part of the game and it is sensible to use a fine tippet and avoid shiny, flashy hooks or brighter colours if the fish are playing hard to get.

Leader Set-Up

Leader set-ups can be another source of confusion. The oft-cited 18ft plus leader which a trout fisherman might use for a team of nymphs is way too long for a fish that will seldom ever move more than an inch or two with a fly. A shorter 9–12ft leader seems more suitable – and where clarity isn't great, a shorter leader is likely to produce not only clearer indications, but a more direct contact on the strike.

The choice is yours, but a good general rule is to use a longer leader in clearer water where fish are spookier and you can spot the fish taking directly; but

This fine roach of 1lb 9oz took a wet fly with surprising aggression, barging its way through smaller fish to make a grab.

Perfect territory for sight fishing – a summer's day on the Taunton-to-Bridgwater Canal. With midges abundant on the water, the roach were highly receptive to small, dark flies.

The Varied Life of the Roach

Few fish species are as widespread as the roach and hence there is no 'one size fits all' approach to catching them. From clear water lakes to little streams and ponds, they all have their own habits and idiosyncrasies.

At the tamer end of the spectrum we have small lakes and the proliferation of man-made day ticket fisheries. These may not appeal to the diehard traditionalist but many are packed with hungry roach and they do offer almost guaranteed bites and a fair introduction to the sport.

The roach are not always of the small and stunted variety either and some more mature venues offer quality as well as quantity.

go shorter when water is murkier and you want a more direct connection because you can't see taking fish with the naked eye.

An indicator is another sensible option where sight fishing is difficult or impossible and a team of three or even more nymphs can be presented beneath a sight bob, which should be the smallest you can get away with. Spiders are excellent for this work. Try a heavier nymph on the point to sink and straighten the leader, with smaller, wispier artificials on your droppers and strike at any movement.

Flies for Roach

These cultivated waters can be fished with nymphs or dries. With water commonly cloudy, dries may well be your only chance of direct, visual fishing. Sometimes you'll see fish basking or patrolling on hot days. They make short work of small dry flies or emergers. The downside is that you are likely to catch only smaller fish this way, unless you can locate larger silver fish on the surface, usually on balmy summer days.

The more likely scenario is nymph fishing. Traditional it is not, but sinking flies with enough colour to stand out (white, yellow or even red) are effective. These should be fished on a fairly short, say 9ft, leader for directness on the strike,

A nice hand-sized fish, great fun on a four weight set-up.

with or without an indicator. Even the more stark day ticket lakes will have some fly life, but the fish are also well accustomed to finding bait.

Simple flies that resemble maggots will work for obvious reasons and if nothing else you will gain some good striking practise for the more challenging waters later.

Roach on Strike

Strike at any unusual movement, paying close attention to the leader and fly line; the leader nudging forward or simply

TEAM WORK

Where sight fishing is tricky, a team of suitable wet flies is the answer. Some exponents have used up to a dozen spiders or tiny nymphs; I find anything more than three quite excessive, not to mention more prone to weeding and tangling. As with a trout set-up, it makes sense to place the heaviest fly of the team on the point, to keep everything straight and tidy.

pausing too long as the fly sinks may be all the indication you receive.

Moving on to more natural still waters, places such as clear lakes, drains and rustic canals can offer delightful, more visual sport. Whilst the fish will be cagier here, you will generally have fewer problems with bite detection, provided you remember a pair of polarising glasses and move to locate the fish. Although these waters will have a far better array of aquatic life to imitate, simple generic patterns such as the Daiwl Bach or even traditionals such as a small Black Pennell should generate some interest.

It is one of the curious aspects of roach, and also rudd fishing, that the above average size fish may prove far more catchable than the many tiddlers you'll spot, which can flatly ignore the fly. This is perhaps because they are still preoccupied with minute food items and even a small artificial is rather a large mouthful. Whatever the case, don't lose heart and you might find that a half pounder takes your fly far more enthusiastically.

Roach are less willing than rudd to rise for dry flies, but given the right conditions they can become quite catchable in this manner. Sunny conditions and evenings especially can yield delightful sport, but the usual rules of engagement apply: use a fine, degreased tippet, avoid dropping a fly line directly over the shoal and deliver the fly gently with as few back casts as possible.

Silver on the Stream

Stillwaters may dominate today's coarse fishing, but in the minds of many roach enthusiasts the species' spiritual home is on the river. Personally, I have struggled with larger rivers and those sorts of water which might be tackled with a swim feeder or heavy stick float. The smaller, shallower rivers are far more manageable however and the fishing in places such as

Roach sometimes struggle to inhale large or bulky flies. A sparsely-dressed, leggy fly is ideal – this roach fell to a size 14 Black Spider.

Roach thrive in many different environments from small streams to big lakes. Even urban rivers (above) usually hold reasonable populations.

mill streams and little tributaries can be highly rewarding.

Flowing water is undoubtedly more demanding to read and understand, but shallow rivers also offer some distinct advantages to the roach angler.

Dry fly fishing is also a distinct possibility in warm weather. Wading makes it easier to find casting space, while the constant movement of the water makes presentation and bite detection easier in many respects.

Unlike their stillwater cousins, river roach cannot study the fly for too long but must make a decision to take or avoid it. And equally, because the progress of the fly and leader is halted when a fish takes, spotting bites is easier if still not strictly easy.

Be warned though, roach and especially the decent samples will not always rise or shift any great distance to seize a fly, hence the need to present a fly at just the right depth which usually means close to the bottom for the fair sized fish. Allow your roach a meal with an absolute minimum of effort and you're more likely to be rewarded.

Head Start for Trout-Fishers

Another blessing for river fishers is the healthy degree of crossover in terms of fly patterns that the trout fisher will already be familiar with. River roach are especially keen on various nymphs and that staple of even poor habitats, the freshwater shrimp. Indeed, flies such as Czech nymphs or a Hare's Ear will all work well in smallish sizes. Trout anglers perhaps have a head start with roach, a species which in spite of its placid appearance does like a decent flow of water.

Roach are very occasionally predatory. Lance Downes took this one on a small, flashy pike streamer!

Larger roach have even been known to share swims with grayling and barbel, clearly no strangers therefore to pacey water.

Other areas worth trying include spots such as weirpools, which have formed some of the most interesting of all my own experiments with roach on the fly. Traditionally, roach were caught on weirs with trotted silkweed and the method can be just as effective if less fashionable today.

Silkweed is simple to copy at the vice; a small clump of marabou or well combed fibres of green dubbing produce a basic but effective fly. The real issue is getting it down to the fish, which often sit just off the weir sill. You have two main options here – either a split shot, or another, heavier 'sacrificial' fly to give added weight.

The sheer variety of roach fishing is the challenge and charm of the exercise. The field is wide open with this unpredictable fish which can bite painfully shyly one day and yet chase the fly energetically or do something utterly unexpected the next. Most bizarrely of all, an angler I was guiding one spring took a roach on a small, glittery pike fly – not that I would recommend this as a likely method!

Try it Out!

With broad tastes and such a wide variety of habitats there is still great scope for experimentation with roach flies. Fishing the Wandle with urban angling friend Theo Pike, for example, the unexpected star of the show was a little pink shrimp. Was this curiosity at play, or the regular introduction of maggots from local kids?

On numerous other occasions I've seen roach picking through weed with little pulls and sucks. Are these fish eating the weed itself, or seeking out life forms hiding therein – or both? It seems that any small and edible-looking discovery is likely to be taken by these curious feeders - and often the simplest tan or coloured bug does the trick.

My own trials continue with flies. Often a simple colour or size change seems to work better than trying to copy the minutiae of nature. The moral for the roach angler is simply to keep a well-stocked fly box and an open mind. Enjoy your own experiments with this fascinating fish.

Roach are beautiful, intriguing quarry for the flyfisher. Wherever you find them their diet and habits vary, testing the angler's adaptability and reflexes.

ROACH FLIES

GRIFFITHS' GNAT

Hook: Dry Fly 14-22
Thread: Fine black
Hackle: Palmered grizzle cock
Body: Black peacock
Tail (optional): a touch of yellow or pearl yarn

An excellent all-round dry fly for still water or stream. A few flies right at the smallest end of the spectrum, down to 20s, can be useful for those occasions when fish are picking off tiny items.

QUILL BUZZER

Hook: Buzzer size 12-16
Thread: Fine tan
Cheeks: Strips from a crisp packet
Body: Stripped peacock quill

Some general buzzer patterns can be handy for roach but go for natural body materials and be prepared to scale down in size from the typical trout versions. Adding CDC or loose dubbing to the head is a good dodge for fish higher in the water.

SILK WEED
(pictured wet)

Hook: Wet fly 10-16
Thread: Green
Body: Marabou or fine, well-teased dubbing in a suitable darkish green

So simple, but worthy of experimentation in those times of the season you suspect roach are feeding heavily on the real thing. Try to get a reasonable colour match to existing weed, bearing in mind that materials darken when wet. Just like the old textbooks described, only minus the stick float!

RED & WOODCOCK SPIDER

WALKER'S OLIVE NYMPH

Hook: Medium nymph 12-20
Thread: Red
Hackle: Two turns of woodcock
Thorax: Peacock
Body: Red thread
Rib: Fine gold wire

Spiders are very useful for roach. They are more easily sucked in by small, sensitive mouths than stiff hackled flies and possess excellent movement even in flat calm conditions. Where sight fishing is impossible, several can be used beneath a small indicator.

Hook: Wet fly 14-16
Thread: Olive
Tail/body: Dyed olive pheasant tail
Thorax: Seal's fur
Rib: Fine gold tinsel

This is the pattern Richard Walker favoured for roach fishing. He recommended it should be 'ribbed with the narrowest gauge flat gold tinsel.' A very useful general nymph.

BLACK PENNELL

Hook: Wet fly 14-18
Thread: Black
Hackle: Black hen
Body: Black floss
Rib: Silver tinsel
Tail: Golden pheasant tippet

An oldie but worth trying in smaller sizes for still water roach. Be sure to include some smaller sizes, right down to 16s and 18s. Resist the temptation to keep twitching, but simply let the fly drift and hang in the water for best results.

Ben Garnett tackles a shallow flow, a typical place for dace.

DACE

The dace is either a delightful little fish or a pesky nuisance; it all depends on your outlook and, dare I say it, whether you have the soul of a poet or a bricklayer. For most of us though, dace provide some welcome, light-hearted fun. These pretty, shoaling river fish tend to favour fast, shallow water and are distinguished from roach by their slimmer-bodied appearance and smaller size.

They are common in many rivers, favouring those pacey reaches also loved by trout and chub. What they lack in size, they make up for in speed and glittering bluish silver colours.

In many ways dace are a perfect fly rod quarry. They're not particularly fussy, but will test the quickest reflexes; they're not big or strong but provide fine, flippant sport on light tackle. 'Light tackle' should perhaps be specified here as the daintiest, most weightless little toothpick of a rod you can lay your hands on; a one or even zero weight outfit is a fun prospect.

Dace do exist in big, wide rivers and even deep, muddy tidal stretches such as my local Exe. These are about the last place you would probably choose to target them however and for more intimate sport the fly caster should head for a small-to-medium sized river with plenty of fast, shallow glides.

Perhaps my favourite dace water is a little mill leat which feeds a much larger river. Typically 2–3ft deep and with a steady current, the waters are full of

---

DACE TACKLE & SEASON

TACKLE: A light, crisp and responsive rod is best for dace, not only for sporting reasons but to hit lightning fast bites! A 7-8ft rod in the 1-4wt bracket is ideal. Floating line is all you need.

Leaders: 8-12ft depending on casting space. Tippets of 2-3lb are suitable.

Other: Waders, fine forceps or a disgorger. Perhaps some coffee or other performance-enhancing drug to sharpen reactions!

SEASON: Traditional coarse season (June-March), but for best sport and the chance to catch on dry flies, summer and early autumn are best. Can be caught on small nymphs through the winter.

playful dace. When sunny, you can watch whole squadrons of these sparkling silver fish in the water. They take a fly beautifully. They also spook easily and a chain reaction often ensues. Scare one fish and it will flash a warning to its shoal mates, who quickly lose their appetites. As with chub therefore, it is a case of creeping one step at a time and making a minimum of false casts.

Flies for Dace

Nymph or dry fly works for these dashing dace, provided you use something small enough. A good starting approach is to use a simple but effective New Zealand set-up of a small dry fly plus a little nymph suspended on 2ft or so of fine tippet tied directly to your dry fly hook. Hook sizes should be small (typically 18-24) for good reason: the dace has a dainty mouth and a propensity to spit out anything suspicious double quick.

A small offering, such as a skinny, leggy nymph (spiders are excellent), may just be taken that split second longer so you can set the hook. I also tend to avoid stiff hackled patterns for the simple reason that dace struggle to inhale them. Soft materials such as CDC are much better for your dries, whilst I replace the cock hackles on flies such as the Black Gnat with softer hen.

Dace may not often be fussy regarding fly choice, but they will sometimes get preoccupied with tiny food items. Look out for dainty rise forms, which can be so tiny you could be forgiven for blaming minnows or missing the signs

altogether. When the fish are picking off minuscule prey items such as aphids or caenis, a size 18 suddenly appears clumsy and I recommend a few micro patterns in the box, which can be invaluable.

Low, clear water and tiny dry flies

are one scenario, but a river carrying extra colour represents a different challenge. Dace are curious fish, and a few patterns with a little extra panache are worth a try when clarity is less than ideal. A Red-bodied spider or even tiny bugs and

Small, clear waters such as mill races, tributaries and chalkstreams make a perfect, intimate setting for the dace. This is also the territory to enjoy sport with the finest tackle you own – a one weight wouldn't be undergunned.

151

Goldheads with a hint of flash are good alternatives to the usual suspects.

If you thought small brown trout were fast on the take, dace are another case entirely. Hitting wet fly takes is easier than those lightning fast rises to dries, where a ratio of a fish every six bites can be an outstanding return! If nothing else, it's excellent reflex training for when you turn your hand back to trout on small dries.

Even if you turn out to be a real dab hand at dace fishing, you are unlikely to win any bragging rights for your exploits. A half pounder is a cracking dace, a one pounder the fish of a lifetime. Perhaps this explains why the species is about as popular as the Natural Law Party.

Go small and soft-hackled for this quick hitter. Connecting with one in six bites is a reasonable return on dry flies.

For those who do share a secret love of this outrageously fast and beautifully sleek customer however, one of our best-loved rivers such as the Wye or Stour could produce some fabulous fly-caught dace to a dedicated angler.

For the rest of us though I would recommend finding your inner child with a featherweight rod and a few stolen hours on a cute little stream. Dace fishing is good for the soul – as well as the reflexes.

Dace-spotting on a tributary of the Rive Exe.

DACE FLIES

MICRO F-FLY

Hook: Fine wire 20-24
Thread: Sheer 16/0
Body: Fine green dubbing
Wing: A few CDC fibres

Tiny dry flies are very useful for fish picking off tiny morsels. This little devil makes a passable aphid impression, having proved a real frustration saver on small, well-bushed streams. A black version is also handy.

MICRO PTN

Hook: Barbless nymph size 18-24
Thread: Fine brown
Legs/thorax: Tiny pinch of hare's ear dubbing
Body & tail: Pheasant tail fibres
Rib: Fine copper wire

Small skinny nymphs fit the bill perfectly for the dace; why not try this trout classic in appropriately small sizes?

A quick bite and another dace. Note the concave rear edge to the dorsal fin, which helps to distinguish it from a small chub.

BLACK SPIDER

Hook: Barbless nymph size 18–24
Body: Black thread
Rib: Ultra fine mylar or tinsel
Hackle: Two turns of partridge fibres

Spiders make ideal small river nymphs
– simple to tie, plenty of movement and
easily inhaled by the smallest of dace.

*A slow section on a clear river, fertile ground
to present a nymph for bream.*

BREAM

Another willing feeder but a genuine challenge, the bottom-feeding bream is a species few would consider attempting with flyfishing tackle. In the right circumstances he has little aversion to taking a fly. The lifestyle of this lazy, shoaling fish is the real challenge however: bream often prefer deep water and conditions of low light to feed. Episodes of strangely aggressive behaviour aside, they also seem to be unwilling to chase around for their prey.

The bream angler therefore has the initial task of finding suitable water. Clear waters such as small canals and ponds are one possibility and on these waters I have tried various nymphs. The smaller 'skimmers' of 1lb or less appear far more willing to accept a fly such as a well-sunk Daiwl Bach than their older relatives, which seem to require different tactics

and unless you try a streamer, that usually means a completely static fly.

The species will often browse in the shallow margins of stillwaters early or late in the day, but most of the better bream I've managed on the fly have come from smallish rivers with a clean or stony bottom. Indeed, in spite of the clichés, they don't mind running water and can sometimes be found in those areas where the river slows and trout thin out; yet the bottom remains clear and sandy or gravelly. The slower edges of clear streams have formed most of my successful bream fishing with a fly rod, where the species can be found mooching around away from the main current.

They are hardly eagle eyes, but bream don't seem to have trouble locating a fly and will follow a sinking nymph

---

BREAM TACKLE & SEASON

TACKLE: A 4wt and upwards outfit, floating line.

Leaders: 9-12ft, tippets from 4-5lb strength.

Other: Long handled landing net, forceps.

SEASON: This bottom feeder is most active in the warmer months, on most waters. June-August would be ideal to try, although a mild spring day may also prove worthwhile where permitted.

quite willingly, albeit with all the speed of an injured sheep. I have seldom managed to get one of these pursuers to grasp the nymph in a rush and the trick seems to be to draw the fish close enough, before allowing it to take the fly completely static.

Watch & Wait

A session on a Finnish river seems typical of the experience. I won't pretend I had travelled to Scandinavia purely to catch bream but on slow days when trout weren't interested, little pods of these dark bronze fish quickly caught my eye and began to look increasingly tempting. Very much a game of sight fishing, the exercise seems to involve a good deal more looking than actually casting.

Standing on a hot river bank, I recall long periods of inaction, studying the sandy bottom in clear waters. But every so often large, dark shapes would emerge into view amongst flickering shoals of bleak and roach, cruising gently away from the main flow. A large Goldhead Hare's Ear or Peeping Caddis would be guided carefully, a safe distance in front of the shoal to sink down to their eye level. More often than not, one of the bream would then advance ('race' is probably too enthusiastic a term for a bream) to follow the nymph, which should be drawn momentarily forwards before being simply left to drop onto the bottom.

For anglers used to giving one final tweak of encouragement, bream require some restraint. More often than not on the river, the following bream would casually

River bream seem rather more susceptible to a fly than their stillwater cousins. They don't mind a little flow, but you should give fast currents a miss.

Smaller bream or 'skimmers' often seem more willing to take moving or gently suspended nymphs than the bigger, lazier adults.

stoop down and the nymph would disappear in a little puff of sand and grit! With a fairly big mouth, bream will gobble a fly up decisively so do wait a split second before striking. A four pounder will put a healthy bend in a fly rod with its weight alone, although with minimal speed or raw power you are in little danger of being broken on even light tackle.

Bream are thus not a species to conjure up heart-racing action but where circumstances allow, such sight fishing opportunities are an exciting diversion. Special tackle is not a necessity for this ponderous fighter.

Careful observation and the odd well-aimed cast are the key, as well as the reserve to avoid retrieving at the crucial moment and simply allow the fish to pick up a static nymph. By far the most effective flies for me have been fairly large Goldhead nymphs; the species has better eyesight than the lumbering tench, but still appears to require a fairly large, easily located target. In other parts of Europe, anglers have had success with well weighted Czech nymphs on running water.

Predatory bream?

Similar tactics have been attempted on still waters such as clear lakes and canals, but with only limited success I must add. My hunch is that patterns such as bloodworms, fished nice and slow, could be

159

worth persevering with. Early mornings, when the fish come close in to browse the margins seem the best time to try, when the fish will be browsing on items like snails and various larvae on the bottom. And yet stillwater bream fishing history has another curious phenomena in the success of 'polystickle' flies, originally tied by the late Richard Walker. Were our ancestors smoking something funny when they tried to catch bream on these diminutive fry patterns?

To some extent all coarse fish are predatory at certain times of the year and bream are no exception. Even so, this shouldn't be a cue to go stripping big lures past these sleepy creatures. With a suitable sized, carefully tweaked pattern you may find bream surprisingly receptive. On several occasions, admittedly by accident for the most part, I have caught bream on a Woolly Bugger intended for

trout or perch. These fish were taken fair and square too, with the fly well engulfed. Reservoirs such as Rutland have also produced some large bream to lure anglers. Going out to deliberately target such fish is another matter however.

Spawning phases may provide a further explanation for such unusually bullish behaviour. As bream gather to breed, they will aggressively nip at intruders, which explains their sudden response to a spinner or indeed the provocative movement of a streamer. However, I've also caught the odd 'predatory' bream as late as August, well after spawning.

Unpredictable

I believe that there is far more to discover about bream. I've found their behaviour fairly unpredictable and like tench, they appear to have different 'moods' which

The tantalising sight of a bream shoal on the move. Time to watch and follow the shoal cautiously – if the fish are browsing for food, a weighted nymph placed in their path might be taken.

can render them anywhere on a sliding scale between catchable and bordering on impossible.

Sometimes you see bream shoals basking high in the water in summer for instance. They look tempting, but I've never got one of these lingering fish to take a fly. To my mind the best time to try is when the fish are browsing – not simply on the move, nor sending up great clouds of silt, but moving slowly about and stooping periodically to pick at the bottom.

Surprisingly aggressive at times, bream will even intercept a streamer when in the mood, especially fish close to spawning – like this one.

Few anglers would target bream specifically then, but they are not as difficult as might be imagined, certainly not as hard as tench. The keen-eyed flyfisher armed with a few suitable patterns might just find some interesting fishing when they least expect it. Definitely a species to file under 'catchable'.

Juha Vainio brings a dinner plate-sized bream to the net. The fish followed a hearvy nymph, before taking it static on the bottom.

Skimmer bream and hybrids (pictured here) are susceptible to small nymphs in clear water — if you can get them deep enough.

BREAM FLIES

GOLDHEAD HARE'S EAR

Hook: Shrimp or heavy nymph hook, size 8-14
Thread: Brown or black
Head: Gold bead
Body: Hare's mask, dubbed
Rib: Gold tinsel
Tail & legs: Grey partridge

An effective bream pattern, especially for the slow edges of clear rivers. Try retrieving gently to gain interest – before leaving this one to be gobbled up static.

POLY STICKLE VARIANT

Hook: 6-10 Long shank lure
Thread: Brown
Body: Mylar tinsel over white thread
Back: Brown raffia, wetted and stretched before tying in
Rib: Silver oval tinsel
Throat: Orange chickabou or cock
Tail: Pinch of dark marabou

This blast from the past might seem unlikely, but when the water is rich in fry or when bream get aggressive close to spawning time in early summer, they can respond well to a small streamer pattern. I much prefer the mobility of marabou to traditional tail materials.

TENCH

Of all the fish you might try to catch within these pages, the tench is one of the greatest challenges. Indeed, this handsome, hard-fighting fish of summer demands not only the right approach and appropriate tackle, but also favourable conditions and, dare I add, a touch of luck.

The habits of the tench are perhaps the biggest obstacle to success. A confirmed bottom feeder, it loves weedy and often muddy places. Your first challenge is therefore to find suitable water where you can fish by sight. Shallow canals, drains or clear water lakes such as gravel pits offer the best possibilities. Occasionally you'll even find them on trout waters. Of the meagre two fish I have managed to catch, both came from clear water where effective sight fishing was possible.

Take a look at the small, red eyes of the tench and the barbules on his mouth and you find a further problem for the flyfisher; the species has fairly poor eyesight and it feeds primarily by feel and taste.

The good news here is that the tench is therefore not especially easy to spook! It's true that they can be shy in extremely clear, shallow water, but on some days you could aim a fly right in the middle of a tench shoal and not disperse them.

The bad news is that the species isn't brilliant at locating a fly. We can help ourselves by using fairly large offerings here – a generously dressed size 8 Stick Fly is a typical offering. But the challenge is often one of dropping a fly so sweetly in the path of the fish that it can be readily

---

TENCH TACKLE & SEASON

TACKLE: A 6wt and upwards outfit, floating line.

Leaders: Tench are not hugely shy of leaders, so 9-10ft is adequate. They are powerful however, and tippets should be no lighter than 5lb.

Other: Forceps, tungsten putty to help sink lighter flies. A tough, long handled landing net is crucial where weed dominates.

SEASON: This bottom feeder is most active in the warmer months, on most waters. June-August would be ideal to try, although a mild spring day may provide easier, less weedy fishing where rules allow.

gobbled up and is almost harder to refuse than to take.

Perhaps the biggest obstacle is in the mind, however. Confidence is so important in any fishing and you must convince yourself if you are to convince the fish. On some occasions however, the tench appears a distinct possibility – it only takes one decent presentation and you may be pleasantly surprised.

One late summer afternoon some time ago stands out as a case in point. I had brought along a fly rod to join a couple of friends who were spinning for pike. The usual jacks simply weren't interested and so I had scaled down to enjoy catching some rudd and roach. My companions were intrigued and on spotting a small tench cruising the margins had issued me a challenge – I was more likely to take it on a fly than a spinner in any case, was their verdict. More in hope than anticipation I watched the dark fish browsing slowly along the bottom. I tied on a small, slow sinking nymph and cast well ahead of the tench. As the fish neared the fly I drew very gently to bring it into position. To my surprise, the tench then sucked in the nymph with no hesitation whatsoever. This is the enigma of tench though – out of many dozens of similar casts I have had only occasional interest.

Mission Possible!

Although frustrating at times, the tench is definitely a catchable fish on fly. You only need look at his diet to find quite a diverse range of invertebrates, from bloodworms

A clear gravel pit. Suitable territory to cast a fly for browsing tench in clear water. Early morning is perhaps the best time, when fish will come close in to undisturbed margins.

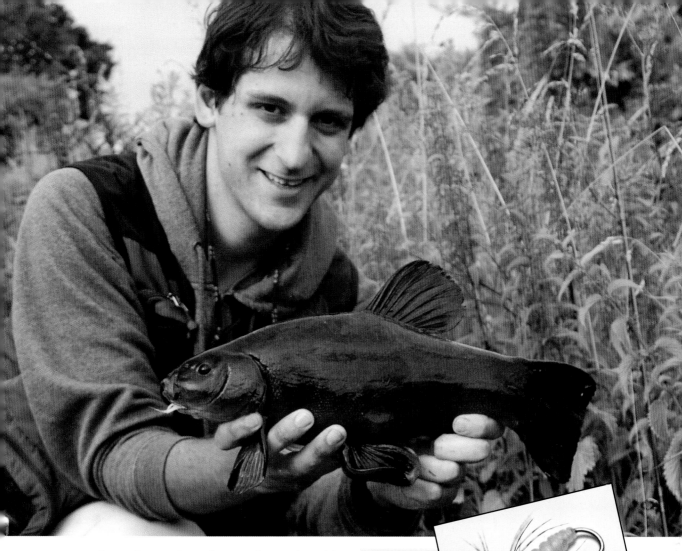

through to damsel nymphs and caddis larvae. Indeed, on clear weedy waters you will sometimes hear bait fishermen complain that the tench are proving elusive because they are preoccupied with natural food.

The best time to try for tench is therefore when they are actively browsing around weed and gravel for food. Early mornings are a particularly likely time in high summer, although I've watched tench actively feeding as early as March. For practical purposes I put my faith in fairly large nymphs, often in a colour that contrasts with the bottom, and cast to these

Tench aren't famed for their great eyesight, so offer a large juicy nymph. You could try a large, dark natural, but I've had more success with flies which contrast with the bottom.

fish as they are busy investigating.

Nymphs are always taken static in my experience. A slow sinking fly can be twitched into the path of a tench and then left to settle – like a natural which has darted from its shelter and settled again on the bottom. For all those infuriating times when the fly is flatly ignored (and there will be many!) you're looking for that 'eureka!' moment when the fly is neatly taken. You may only receive one chance in many casts so you should strike with care, giving the tench a second to engulf the bait properly without pulling your artificial straight out of its big, gaping mouth.

The Tricky Tench Take

Earning a take can be tricky in itself, but is by no means the end of the challenge.

The tench is a powerful fish and one to really test a fly rod; I've lost more than I've ever caught. It can be tempting to try lighter lines when the fish are not taking, but tench have fairly poor vision and I'm inclined to believe it makes little difference and it is unwise to go below a tippet strength of 5lb breaking strain. If dense weed is present, you could go heavier – and a micro barbed hook is advisable too, since barbless models can

Where water clarity is an issue, a 'bait' fly along with some loose feed might be your only viable option.

This pretty little tench took a slow-sinking nymph wth no hesitation whatsoever. If only it was always that easy.

quickly come adrift when fish burrow into weed (a lesson I've learned the hard way!)

The quicker route to success might be to use a 'bait fly' such as a piece of imitation bread, corn or maggot, but for many flyfishers this simply isn't the same challenge and is little different from using conventional coarse fishing tackle.

Bait anglers have long noticed that tench seem to pick out objects which contrast with the bottom – more evidence in favour of using a large, contrasting nymph. And if you are really struggling to interest the tench you could try infusing your artificial with some scent such as lobworm extract or a sweet flavour.

Whichever way you look at it, tench are a challenge. You need the right water, foraging fish and tackle with some power in reserve. Nevertheless, the species is definitely another to file under 'possible'.

TROUBLESOME TINCAS

Is there a more frustrating fish than the tench to catch on fly tackle? The answer is probably yes, but the tench must be near the top of the list. We know for a fact that tench do eat all sorts of natural goodies, but most of the interest I've had seems to have been with white or lightly coloured flies- perhaps provoking a reaction more to do with curiosity than natural feeding. This also chimes with the accounts of others, who have caught fish from waters such as estate lakes using large, contrasting nymphs.

Another observation seems to be that the smaller, younger tench react in much livelier fashion to flies. Does the eyesight of the fish deteriorate with age? Does the diet of the tench change during its life span? I've cast so close to big passing tench, the fish have virtually been tripping over the nymph - or wearing the thing like a bloody hat. Perhaps this is why it feels so gratifying when you finally manage to land your tench, whatever the size.

TENCH FLIES

STICK FLY

Hook: Size 8 long nymph or caddis
Thread: Dark brown
Tail: Bright synthetic fibres
Body: Dyed black peacock herl
Hackle: Claret partridge fibres

One of very few flies to gain interest from tench. Try this in large sizes and sink close to the bottom before leaving static as the fish comes near. I prefer a soft hen or partridge hackle to cock – it has a better 'feel' and sinks quicker.

POLAR FLAKE

Hook: Carp hook, size 8-10
Thread/head: Bright orange
Body: Polar fibres or marabou

If all else fails, a bait-style fly is a good option. This one stands out well to a passing fish.

HEAVY GRUBBER

Hook: Heavyweight nymph, size 6-10
Thread: Brown
Body: The rim from a latex glove
Thorax: Peacock herl
Hackle: Two turns of grey partridge

Browsing tench will investigate light-coloured objects presented on the bottom. This fly is loosely based on the 'Grub Fly', also found in this book.

BARBEL

Not a fish for the faint-hearted, or indeed the impatient, barbel represent an exciting challenge to the fly caster. The act of hooking one requires a dedicated effort, and that's even before the hair-raising task of taking on the brute strength and tenacity of a hooked fish. Few river residents will give you such a dogged encounter on a 6wt outfit. To make a comparison, a fresh-run 10lb salmon may go ballistic, leaping athletically and moving in all directions when hooked. But a barbel fights with cunning; unlike the flashy new arrival, he knows every hole and snag on the river.

Those still convinced that barbel are fish which are only caught using sweet corn and boilies should perhaps take to heart the words of Bob James, my own mentor in the thorny task of taming barbel on a fly rod. He recalls trips with John Bailey to a wild River Wye where the penny dropped for these pioneers of barbel flyfishing.

'It's always funny when people raise eyebrows at the thought of flyfishing for barbel,' he smiles. 'On the Wye back in the late 70's we encountered fish that had grown to large sizes entirely on natural food,' he recalls. 'We couldn't get them to feed on anything – and of course, they'd never seen luncheon meat in their lives! We quickly realized we should have been flyfishing with nymphs.'

You only need look at the physique of the barbel to find a creature tailor-made for foraging on the bottom in fast flows. The powerful, muscular body is

---

BARBEL TACKLE & SEASON

TACKLE: A 10ft rod rated 6wt or above is the ideal tool for the job. The sheer power of the species demands a quality blank with plenty of power and flex.

Leaders: A rod's length of 8lb fluorocarbon or tough mono. Avoid knotted leaders or light line: any weakness in your tackle will quickly be discovered!

Other: Tungsten putty or split shot to add extra weight to flies. Waders are also essential to get close to the fish.

SEASON: June-September are the best months, with the fish especially active right at the start of the season.

simply built for thriving in the current, the low-slung mouth adept at engulfing a wide range of invertebrates and even small fish. The whiskers also indicate a fish that feeds by feel perhaps more than sight, hence the need to land flies close enough to solicit a reaction.

The typical size of an adult fish should also leave the reader in no doubt as to the appetite of the species. Caddis larvae, freshwater shrimp and mayfly nymphs are particular favourite meals, the latter being gorged with frenzied abandon when hatching, sadly before the start of the coarse fishing season, it must be added.

Barbel Water

As with many flyfishing adventures, perhaps the first challenge is simply finding suitable water to try. Barbel flyfishing is predominantly sight fishing, which

SENSE APPEAL: SCENTED FLIES?

That barbel can see a fly well enough to take it is fact, but out of the main senses of the species, sight comes well behind touch, smell and taste. This allows them to feed even at night or in muddy, floodwater conditions. Could success rates be boosted by using an artificial fly with scent? Barbel expert Bob James suspects so – and has even tried boosting the appeal of his own large nymphs with a special 'dip' of amino acid, with some success. But is it cricket? It's your decision, but experimentation could well be rewarded in this area.

A stubborn, dogged fight is to be expected on a fly rod. One favourite trick is for the fish to sit hard on the bottom, refusing to be moved – play them with caution.

The barbel is a fish tailor-made for scouring the river bed. A close, controlled presentation right on the deck is your best chance of action.

demands the right conditions: namely, clear water and good visibility. Coloured water or raised river levels invariably make the task all but impossible.

Find yourself a stony, clear river where you can sneak up on the fish, however, and you have an excellent chance of action. Quite often barbel can be seen turning and moving across the flow in such conditions, sometimes even rolling onto their sides. Coarse anglers once speculated that these movements were caused by the fish kicking up stones with their tails; a more likely explanation is that they are taking nymphs.

Close-Quarter Fishing

Trying for barbel on a fly rod has more in common with close range wet fly methods such as Czech Nymphing than traditional trout fishing. One aspect in the angler's favour is that barbel don't seem to spook easily and provided you advance carefully, it's possible to get very close to the fish. When feeding hard, they will sometimes literally swim around the angler's wading boots with little sign of alarm!

Wading is essential, and certainly spooks fewer fish than approaching from a high bank. They point their noses into the flow, so you must approach them from behind. Don't start casting until you have a secure position near to the fish, with as

175

A solid fish for a relieved author, after a hair-raising fight in rocky weter.

much of the flow behind you as possible. This can be vital if you hope to guide a heavy nymph accurately towards their position and not have your fly simply dragged out off kilter.

On this note it's worth remembering that fast flowing water can be deceptive to the casual observer. We naturally assume that the river flows at the pace of the surface, when in fact the current will be considerably slower deeper in the water column, where the nymph must be presented. This is why it is important to try and use as little fly line on the water as possible. The more line on the water, the more your presentation is at the mercy of the surface current. Sometimes barbel will accept a moving nymph trundled just off the bottom. More often it is a case of getting the fly to settle

on the deck momentarily, just in front of a fish, before gently drawing it forward to induce the take.

In theory it sounds simple. The reality can be very different in a healthy push of water and with several big fish lying nearby. They will seldom shift any distance to grab a nymph, so accuracy is important.

Currents need to be taken into account at all times, giving enough space for the fly to reach the fish correctly. Barbel are no strangers to fast flows and even a well-weighted fly can sail frustratingly past the target. This is one reason why fluorocarbon leaders are favoured – but also why it's a good idea to bring some additional weight in a pocket. Split shot will do the job, but I much prefer tungsten

This fish took a Peeping caddis – specific fly choice is less key than having something well-weighted, teased right in front of a hungry mouth.

putty, which won't kink line and can be added in any quantity either on the nose of the fly or a few inches up the leader.

Unless the barbel are tapping into a particularly abundant food source, it's debatable whether the specific fly pattern makes any big difference. Opinion is divided as to whether a dark or light nymph shows up better to the fish. Most importantly, it must be designed along practical lines to present properly in a healthy flow of water. You'll notice that some flies use dumbbell eyes and even small jig-type heads to get down to the fish quickly and avoid snagging bottom.

Battles with Barbel

If getting takes from barbel wasn't enough of a challenge, the business of taming one on light tackle is an issue in itself. They are powerful, stubborn fighters that will give you one of the toughest battles you've ever encountered on a fly rod. Rule number one is to avoid the temptation to drop line strengths in an effort to get more takes. Barbel are not especially line shy, but they are extremely tough fighters; couple this with the typically stony and pacy water they thrive in and you have a very demanding scenario.

If the angler has one advantage, it's that barbel don't spook too readily. Wade as close as you can and presentation becomes easier.

This Wye fish came from a group of several spotted in a clear run.

Rocket from the Wye! Weight for weight, perhaps no other fish will give you such a hair-raising battle on a 6wt.

Keeping the rod tip high provides maximum flex in the early stages of the fight, which can develop from an almost nonchalant, ploughing movement to weighty, determined runs. A quality rod which refuses to 'lock up' is a definite advantage here. Modern carbon blanks are brilliant to counter the fight and some of the newer models employing super-flexible carbon, such as the Hardy Sintrix, are ideal for this task.

Besides careful playing it is also important to release the fish carefully, especially when the fight has been hard. Always hold fish upright into the current, only releasing it when it regains strength.

The Quirks of the Barbel

Some other barbel habits are also worth noting if you're to avoid disaster with a hooked monster. One peculiar trend is their habit of 'sulking' on the bottom. The body shape and sheer weight of the fish make it possible for a barbel to simply clamp itself in position across the flow using its low profile and large fins. You might easily assume the fish had become snagged fast, such is the doggedness of this tactic.

When faced with this situation, avoid the temptation to apply more and more force; if the barbel suddenly shifts, you could be smashed in an instant and I've lost barbel in this manner on heavy legering tackle, never mind a fly rod. A better course of action is to change the angle of the line, wading downstream of the fish until it moves again. Another solution, provided you are using a barbed hook, is to slacken off the pressure a little, but not too severely, so that you can carefully feel the line and be ready once the fish runs free again.

As with other species, fishing pressure can have quite a large bearing on how barbel respond to anglers. Where large quantities of bait are routinely introduced, the habits of the fish may change. Nevertheless, barbel will still eat natural food and the first few weeks of the season from mid-June onwards, when the fish have been living and feeding undisturbed, represent probably the best chance of sport. I'm not about to argue with the experience of Bob James in any case, who is a firm believer that the barbel are more inclined to take a moving, natural offering in the early summer.

Aggressive Takes to the Fly

More surprising still is the aggressive behaviour of the fish in the early season which may go some way to explaining the occasional and accidental capture of big barbel by anglers fishing salmon flies. Bob himself has caught them on streamers, quite by design. Barbel certainly do eat small fish species and fry, especially when they represent easy food. 'They can be very predatory,' Bob comments, 'particularly when the minnows are spawning.'

Mayfly time is another golden opportunity, although access to many rivers is limited. The fish push well up some river systems however, and when the fish are feeding hard on game angling beats (ie clearly eating and not spawning!) I see no reason why the flyfisher shouldn't try his or her luck – indeed some huge fish have been taken by anglers during this period of abundance.

Barbel tackle must be up to the job. Bob favours tough leaders and the extreme flex of a Hardy Sintrix fly rod.

Tough stuff – the business end of a seven-pounder.

Walker's Mayfly Nymph is a great choice for barbel. These well-leaded versions are the work of expert Bristol flytyer John Horsfall.

A well-leaded Walker's Mayfly nymph seems like the obvious choice – although Bob has taken these mayfly-gorging fish on a dry fly. With the overslung mouth of the species, you can imagine the ungainly, almost vertical angle of the rise in this most bizarre of sights!

Barbel Overseas

Barbel fishing abroad seems even stranger to intrepid travelling anglers in Europe who witness barbel regularly taken on local methods that would appear to border on insanity. Spain holds several species of barbel, with some exciting and unusual prospects for the fly angler. On some of these rivers, barbel respond best of all to dry fly tactics! Other barbel show a decidedly aggres-sive streak and are regularly taken on fairly large Streamers. Those curious to learn more should track down some of Bob James and John Bailey's intriguing work on the subject.

Back she goes...

A barbel on the Wye

Bob James' barbel flybox

WALKER'S MAYFLY NYMPH

Hook: Size 8, longshank nymph
Thread: Brown
Underbody: Lead wire
Tail: Pheasant tail fibres
Body: Cream coloured wool
Rib: Tying silk
Thorax cover & legs: Pheasant tail fibres

During and even outside the mayfly hatch, this fly is worth a go for barbel. It both sinks and shows up beautifully in the water. You may want to add even more lead wire than you might for your trout patterns.

EP MINNOW

DUMB-BELL NYMPH   PEEPING CADDIS

Hook: Low water salmon hook, size 6–8
Eyes: Lead dumb-bell eyes
Tail: Pheasant tail fibres
Body: Olive dubbing
Rib: Gold wire
Thorax: Hare's ear or any coarse, dark dubbing
Legs: Partridge
Thorax cover: Pheasant fibres

This is a darker, general-fit pattern. Designed to sink quickly and fish hook point up, it's another suitable candidate for barbel and useful where the bottom is snaggy.

Hook: Longshank nymph
Head: Tungsten bead
Thread: Dark brown
Body: Spectrablend dubbing, dark hare's ear
Eyes: Antron fibres, burnt with a lighter
Legs: Partridge fibres

Caddis are staple food for barbel. This pattern is not only a reliable copy, but with the addition of a tungsten bead it quickly gets down to the fish. Ugly to cast, but most useful.

EP MINNOW *dressing*

Hook: Long shank lure, size 4–8
Head: Eyed dumb-bell head, tied to flip hook 'point up'
Body: Olive, brown & white ep fibres, plus a hint of flash material
Markings: Pantone pen or sharpie marker

Barbel are no strangers to eating minnows; on the contrary they are easily capable of overpowering these hapless creatures, which can represent a plentiful food source. Hence it's well worth keeping a few suitable streamers in the fly box, especially in the early season when the barbel are preying on them.

Virtually any fish is catchable on fly gear — if you're crazy enough to go there!

OTHER SPECIES

We have dealt with most of the usual suspects as far as coarse fish go – but naturally, there are many other possibilities worth mentioning. Almost every species can be tempted with a fly at some point in the year, although you would have to be slightly unhinged to habitually try for some of the fish which populate this section of the book.

The ethos of flyfishing is all about the challenge, however, not only the result. It should be about possibilities and not arbitrary boundaries. The chances are, if you've thought of it, some maniac (sorry, I mean 'enthusiast') has done it. Flyfishing for eels anyone?

Mini Species

There is a prevalent tendency in angling to decry all of the smaller fishes as 'nuisance' species. This is a shame, because if nothing else they make for interesting sub-plots on any day out, offering some flippant fun and grounding us with memories of our more innocent days of childhood.

MINNOWS were as much a part of my own formative years as penny sweets or kick-abouts in the park. Found in large numbers in many rivers, these pretty olive and gold fish will eagerly nibble at a small nymph, giving little judders that

we sometimes mistake for bigger residents. Even a size 18 looks big beside a minnow – which is probably merciful, unless you want to catch a few, in which case some tiny size 20 or smaller Hare's Ears or spiders will catch effortlessly. If nothing else, a good head of minnows suggests plenty of fodder for trout, chub and perch. An olive and gold Streamer could be a killer where you find minnows by the score.

GUDGEON are another small boys' favourite. A confirmed bottom-hugger, they will take small weighted nymphs trundled right on the deck. As will the Bullhead, also known as the sculpin or miller's thumb, if you scale flies right down. Again, few would want to catch them, but they are a cute fish to add to your list of species, and also prime food for predators.

BLEAK are another pretty fish – pretty annoying to most. They form huge shoals on rivers and some canals and will willingly take just about any tiny dry or wet fly you throw at them. For some instant gratification – or to entertain a youngster for half an hour – they offer a quick fix of fun. They are also another good staple prey item and a good indicator. On one occasion I recall taking several on a PTN, largely because my companion had forgotten to bring any zander bait.

Minnow

Bleak

Gudgeon

RUFFE are a curious near-relation of the perch. I've never tried, but with their greedy mouths, those small lures and nymphs so deadly for their striped cousins ought to work a treat.

Bigger Challenges

Some fish are covered only in passing within these pages for the simple reason that they are either too narrow in their distribution, or poorly suited to fly tackle – or both! Not that you should ever say never, because usually there is a way.

HYBRIDS are crosses between fish species, most commonly a mixture of roach and bream, or roach and rudd. A lot of the rules for the parent species apply and small nymphs will account for hybrids on canals and rivers.

SILVER BREAM are an enigma, and not to be confused with young common bream or 'skimmers'. The species grows

The ruffe is an aggressive little fish for its size, seldom growing to more than about five inches. It is recognisable by its long, spiny dorsal fin and down-pointing mouth.

only smaller and is marked by a larger eye and dark fins. Quite a few day ticket fisheries as well as natural waters have them and their disadvantage is that they prefer to feed on the bottom. For those keen to tick the species off, it could be worth trying some loose feed with maggots or casters to draw the fish up in the water a little then offering a suitable sized wet fly in the mix.

The same could be applied to **CRUCIAN CARP** which are not only bottom feeders, but notoriously picky biters. Throw in their preference for murky ponds and you hardly have a recipe for classic flyfishing. They do occasionally come up in the water to eat, especially if the water is shallow however. Then, a small nymph either

189

fished New Zealand style, or allowed to sink under an indicator might work. A bit of 'cheating' with loose feed could be your answer otherwise, with a suitable fly fished alongside.

GRASS CARP are a more viable target and can be tempted by means similar to those used for commons and mirrors at the surface. Looking almost chub-like, they are designed to feed off the top.

Floating 'bait' flies will work, although the species is naturally a weed browser and I have often wondered whether a simple green fly might work, perhaps something like a larger version of the simple 'silk weed' fly in our roach chapter. Be warned though – grass carp

Ide are terrific fish on a fly rod – beautifully coloured and not overly fussy. They are a school fish, so if you catch one there will probably be others around too.

are notoriously fussy feeders and presentation must be spot on.

Other non-natives include **ORFE, GOLDEN TENCH** and **BROWN GOLDFISH**. Found at day ticket fisheries, these are often well-accustomed to taking floating pellets, bread and other artificial baits. For purists we have probably now reached the point of no return: pleasure seekers of a less hoity-toity variety might well spend a fun hour or two tackling these fish with carp-style flies.

IDE are another fish occasionally found in ponds. But the wild strain, common in many parts of Europe on both rivers and lakes, are a terrific fly rod quarry. These brilliant bronze gold creatures look like a cross between rudd and chub. They are also surprisingly predatory, taking everything from insects to small fish like vendace and bleak. When cast to, they take a fly very well indeed and I've caught them on both weighted nymphs and streamers such as the good old Woolly Bugger.

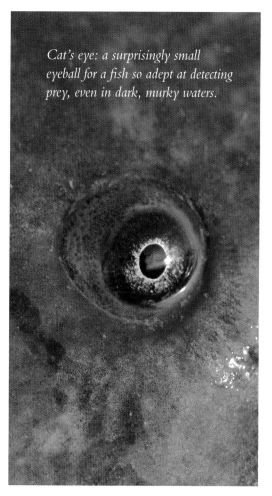

Cat's eye: a surprisingly small eyeball for a fish so adept at detecting prey, even in dark, murky waters.

This way madness lies...

And finally, we have those fishes which even the most ardent flyfisher balks at. Nevertheless, the possibilities are there, should you wish to explore them. Such fishes also raise a wider point: that some species are thought of as 'uncatchable' on the fly largely because nobody is bold (or insane) enough to try. The truth is out there somewhere.

EELS have the sort of eyesight your great grandmother wouldn't be proud of and are probably the last fish many anglers would try to catch by any means, let alone fly. One surprising feature of this interesting species is that while renowned as a short–sighted scavenger, eels will also actively hunt and seize small fish. Might a small bait fish pattern, tweaked slowly near to visible eels be the answer?

It would take a brave (or daft) angler to seriously target eels on the fly. Were I to go for it myself, I would be tempted to soak a fry pattern in fish oil to appeal to the eel's well-developed sense of smell. Call it cheating if you like, but with the eel's poor sight the angler probably needs all the help he or she can get.

WELS CATFISH are another great predator found with increasing regularity in many waters. They are active hunters as well as scavengers and will devour young water birds as well as fish. Lure anglers have caught them on jerk baits, so perhaps a big fly might work?

Bob James is the only angler I know to have tried and his attempt still stands as

legendary in its audacity. One summer day on a large reservoir in Spain he noticed something sinister going on. Located on a valve tower were clusters of nesting martins. Every so often from this precarious position, a fledgling would drop into the lake. There would be a plop, followed by the great swirl as a catfish accepted the free gift.

Nobody believed it, so Bob set about making some special flies "mostly out of any old junk I could find!' he recalls – and

Introducing 'Batman and Robin' – Bob James once narrowly missed out on a spectacular catch with these audacious fledgling imitations.

soon 'Batman and Robin' (above right) were born! He admits that the dynamic duo were 'horrible to cast on a fly rod – totally un-aerodynamic, although every now and again one would sail out perfectly like a model glider.' Nothing happened for a time – until one of the guards at the reservoir who had been watching explained how the catfish seemed to appear as the young fledglings struggled.

'As soon as I added some additional movement, the most phenomenally big mouth came up and engulfed it,' Bob reflects. His trout rod took on a ridiculous bend but sadly the giant wels came off the hook. Perhaps just as well, as it may have taken hours to land.

A great attempt nonetheless and one you really couldn't make up.

HANDY TIPS
and further thoughts

Be Prepared!

It's a situation familiar with many anglers, myself included: you're making your way around the bank when you spot a cracking fish, mooching along without any suspicion whatsoever. It looks like a willing taker and has yet to see you. You get into position, get ready to cast and… the fly line is wrapped around the rod or the fly itself misplaced. By the time you've flipped the line clear and found the fly, the fish is either spooked or gone.

The remedy is simple: always be ready to cast. Many rods have keeper rings or at least a cork handle to retain the fly. Great in theory, but many times, your leader will be as long as or longer than the rod and hence the fly line gets lost in the rod rings – another chance missed as you

faff about! A good dodge here is simply always to ensure the fly line is clear of the tip and you're ready to cast. One way of doing this with a longer leader is to take it around the back of the reel and fasten the fly to a rod ring under light tension *(see photo below)*.

The Brilliant NZ Method

Fishing the 'New Zealand' style dropper, for those too shy to ask, is a simple but deadly way to present both a dry and wet fly together to great effect. A fairly buoyant, easy-to-spot dry fly such as a Klinkhamer is attached to the leader – and a nymph is then suspended underneath on a length of line directly to the bend of the dry fly hook. This presents a wet fly beautifully, especially on running water and effectively hedges your bets.

You may catch on the dry fly, but if a fish intercepts your nymph instead, the floating fly will pull under the surface like a bite indicator. This is a great method for chub or dace on a stream but can also used for suspending nymphs in the upper layers of a stillwater for other species.

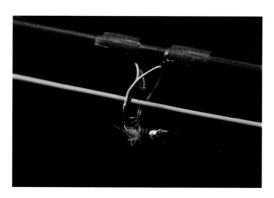

THE PERFECT INDICATOR FLY

Another neat way of turning a dry fly into an indicator is to incorporate a little section of pole float sleeving onto the hook. Simply thread the line through the eye of the fly, then through the sleeve and you have a fully adjustable fly, allowing you to present your nymph at any chosen depth.

You may struggle to hook as many fish on the dry fly – but one way to give the dry fly a 'stopping point' is to incorporate a rig ring into your leader, so that the dry fly will hit this when it slides down the line, and the hook stays in place.

To Wade or Not to Wade?

Perhaps the most underrated item of tackle amongst the coarse angling fraternity is the humble pair of waders. Not only do these allow you to access areas otherwise out of bounds, they also let you get closer to the fish without spooking them.

Standing in the water presents a much lower profile than up on a high bank certainly. It's also often much easier to cast a fly line in the water, free of trees and obstacles on the bank.

The real danger with wading is that of spooking fish. When should you refrain from wading? Only you can make that call but there's no way to 'unspook' fish once you've made a clumsy move. The narrower and shallower the water is, the bigger the risk.

Striking Matters

The matter of when to strike is not entirely straightforward. When the line or an indicator signal a bite, or we clearly see a fish take the fly, the answer is far simpler. Small or quick fishes should be struck instantly (dace, roach etc), whereas the real bucket mouths (carp, tench etc) may need that instant longer before the decisive strike – instant reaction may sometimes pull the hook directly out of the mouth otherwise.

On other occasions you might need to trust your instincts. In semi-clear water with a small fly for example, you can easily lose sight of the fly. Your best guide in such circumstances might be any one of several indicators: the sudden white of a mouth opening, the gobble of lips or a fish accelerating forward before tilting to feed. One rule applies – trust your instincts and if in doubt, strike! What have you got to lose?

It is the same with dry flies. If you lose sight of the target then try to retain a rough idea of its position. If you see a rise in the area then strike. You might miss – but you'll learn a lot by trial and error just observing the fish you want to catch. And remember: you lose nothing by striking!

One final point is that strikes should be appropriate for the size of the fish and the strength of tackle. Whilst you may need to hit the bites of quick-biting silver fish fast, coarse fishers should be aware that most modern fly lines have very little stretch and therefore a simple lift or tightening of the line is usually all that is required. Pike are perhaps the big exception here – their bony jaws require a stronger hook set.

Long or Short Leader?

One question which continually bamboozles both new and old flyfishers is leader length. Each species chapter in this book gives a rough guide, but a few points are worth mentioning here. Is longer always better? Not necessarily. If space is limited, a long leader can be a nightmare. If you're fairly new to fly casting, a longer leader is also harder to handle. Quite often with coarse fish, a rod's length (ie around 9ft) is adequate.

A longer, say 12ft plus leader, really pays off when fish are spooky or the water very clear – casting to chub on an aquarium-clear stretch of river perhaps. This is very different to a murky pond where fish won't easily detect the line. Wherever you fish and whichever leader you use, let the fish see the fly – but not the fly line.

Another reason to use a long leader is to present more than one fly. This is fine for smaller species, but do remember every knot on your leader adds another potential weak spot. Multi-fly leaders (or indeed any leaders knotted in several

places) are a bad idea where big, strong fish such as carp or pike are concerned. Keep it strong and simple!

Mobility is Key

It seems like an obvious point, but on so many levels it pays to be light of foot and really search for your own space. Flyfishing is an excellent method for travelling light, so make the most of this freedom by exploring your chosen water to the full. Not only will you discover areas which others miss, the fish also feel safer and more willing to feed in a natural, undisturbed manner in these quieter places.

A bait angler can try to draw fish to a comfortable area with loose feed. Fly anglers don't often have this advantage and in any case, you should seek out areas where the fish feed and reside naturally. Think about their preferences first, rather than your own!

Fly Positioning and Presentation

The fly angler is essentially trying to offer fish something which doesn't often occur in nature – a free, easy meal. How often does a fly drop conveniently onto a fish's nose? Do prey fish often swim towards predators?

Usually the art of getting a take is in presenting the fly naturally, so it can be seen and taken – but not offered in so blatant a way that your quarry feels suspicious. Even small fish will be suspicious of a fly which drags against the natural course of the current, or lands directly on their heads. One careful delivery is worth a thousand clumsy, ill-considered casts.

Like trout anglers, fly casters in search of river coarse fish almost always wade and cast upstream, or at least across the current. Not only does this avoid unnatural drag, but fish tend to point into the current and will thus hopefully spot the fly long before they spot the angler.

Bait Tactics?

To some purists, the idea of combining fly tackle with bait fishing is sheer blasphemy. To most others, it is just a method like any other, with its own purposes. We have already discussed using 'bait' flies for carp, for example, but there are many other applications too. Is this going too far?

There is certainly something magical about tricking any fish with a natural-looking imitative fly and this is the essential kick of flyfishing. But different scenarios demand different approaches. Take the case of a coloured river, for example – a nymph may be simply lost, whilst some loose-fed sweet-corn or maggots, combined with a suitable look-alike, could turn a blank day into a success. I have successfully caught chub, for example, in this manner on days when

A good rule for all flyfishing is 'let the fish see the fly before they see you!' Even pike spook, so as Ben Garnett shows here, it's worth side casting along the margins before you disturb spots and risk putting your shadow over margin-hugging fish.

Fly line can be a pain on the bank. In this instance, Nigel Savage uses a large net head as a line tray – which also makes it easy to move swims without repeatedly reeling the line back onto the spool.

'natural' flyfishing proved impossible. The fish don't bend the fly rod any less than if you had used a 'proper' fly.

There are even, dare I say it, times when an angler might present real bait using fly tackle. Certainly Richard Walker himself mentions such fishing when tackling painfully shallow swims for roach. In such waters the smallest float or swimfeeder might scare the fish so why not present a maggot with a fly rod? In many ways this is akin to good old-fashioned free-lining but with greater scope for presenting small baits which you couldn't normally cast far enough.

It's not 'true' flyfishing, granted, and to some this would be overstepping the boundaries. But perhaps the whole act of chasing coarse fish with game tackle is all about crossing boundaries! It is my belief that fishing should be about enjoyment and discovery, not about division and elitism. I flyfish because I love it and it works for me – not because I consider it 'more sporting' or raises me above other anglers.

Author of Trout in Dirty Places, Theo Pike, with a fine roach/rudd hybrid – caught on the fly, of course.

NEW HORIZONS

Above all, flyfishing for coarse fish should open up a vast array of new possibilities. The field is wide open on rivers, streams, canals, drains, lochs, reservoirs, ponds, anywhere. Just because it's not 'the done thing', it doesn't mean flyfishing won't work. On the contrary, you may well get that lovely feeling of finding a deadly method nobody else is using.

REALLY USEFUL PATTERNS

The following list is intended as a summary of those fly patterns which have proved their worth time and again for various coarse species. Most are readily available from fishing stockists – and if not, are easy enough to tie. However, it is worth remembering that commercially-available flies tend to be sold in sizes most suited to trout. Not only do dainty feeders such as roach and dace commonly require smaller versions, but for 'big mouths' such as chub and carp, bigger flies may also be useful.

GOLD-RIBBED HARE'S EAR

Hook: Nymph or grub 8-20
Thread: Brown or black
Body: Dubbed hare's mask
Rib: Gold oval tinsel or wire
Tail/legs: Partridge

A fly which truly fits the term 'indispensible', this general pattern is a useful weapon almost anywhere, on running or still water. I prefer this unweighted version for lakes, drains and canals, but on rivers a gold-head version sinks down to the fish better.

Species: Roach, rudd, bream, tench, chub, carp, barbel

FRATNIK'S F-FLY

Hook: 10-24 fine wire
Thread: To suit
Wing: Natural or white CDC
Body: Fine dubbing

The F-fly is another of those innocuous-looking but deadly 'general-fit' flies that no angler should be without, even more so where coarse fish are concerned. They are very easy to tie and fuss-free – no floatant should be applied. Small black versions are brilliant for roach and rudd, whilst chub and carp like a larger F-fly.

Species: Dace, roach, rudd, chub, carp

KLINKHAMER SPECIAL

Hook: Sedge or special Klinkhamer/ emerger hook 10-20
Thread: Brown or black
Hackle: Genetic cock hackle
Wing post: Antron yarn, foam or CDC
Thorax: Peacock or coarse, 'leggy' dubbing
Body: Fine dubbing
Rib: Wire or tinsel

The Klinkhamer is another of those exceptional flies truly worthy of the term 'indispensible' – and not just for trout and grayling. Representing an emerging insect, its success lies in its ease of location – for both fish and angler. It can be tied in a range of sizes and colours although black is especially useful. For smaller mouths however, a large stiff hackle can be hard to suck in, so either scale down or use a softer material such as hen rather than cock.

Species: Roach, rudd, dace, chub, carp

COCH-Y-BONDDU

Hook: Dry fly 10-18
Thread: Brown or Black
Hackle: Reddish brown cock
Body: Peacock herl
Tag: Gold flat tinsel

One for the summer, this generic beetle is another fly in the 'simple but deadly' class. Use with confidence around overhanging cover on either still or running water to represent a fallen natural insect. Especially useful for chub.

Species: Chub, rudd, roach, carp

FOAM BACK BEETLE   BLACK BUZZER

Hook: Wide gape 8-18
Thread: Black
Body: Peacock herl
Hackle: Black cock
Back: Strip of black foam

Hook: Buzzer or shrimp 10-20
Thread: Fine black
Body: Well-varnished thread
Rib: Fine flat tinsel or mylar
Head/cheeks: built up thread/ dyed biot

Another excellent little beetle, this simple foam pattern is durable and useful for various species but especially chub and carp. A little bright yarn can also be added to the back if you're struggling to pick the fly out.

Species: Chub, rudd, carp

Coarse fish eat buzzers as readily as do trout at times, especially on lakes. Best fished with a painfully slow retrieve on a long leader in teams of three or four. Experiment with smaller sizes such as 14-16 for silver fish, and strike at any indication.

Species: Roach, rudd, carp

PHEASANT TAIL NYMPH

CZECH NYMPH

Hook: Nymph 10-20
Thorax: Tiny pinch of hare's mask
Thorax cover: Pheasant or thin skin
Thread: Brown or black
Body & tail: Pheasant tail
Rib: Fine copper wire

The 'PTN' is an especially useful fly for the river angler, although it also works fished like a buzzer on ponds and lakes. Richard Walker himself rated this excellent nymph for roach fishing in smaller sizes.

Species: Roach, rudd, dace, chub

Hook: Shrimp or Grub model 8-16
Thread: Tan or Brown
Underbody (optional): Lead wire
Body rib: Flat tinsel
Back rib: Mono
Shellback: Strip of "thin skin" or similar
Body: Cream dubbing
Head/Legs: Natural hare's mask

No list of river flies would be complete without the Czech Nymph. This is an excellent pattern to present deep for a range of species, but especially chub and roach. European anglers also catch bream, carp and barbel using them.

Species: Chub, roach, barbel, bream

DADDY LONGLEGS

Hook: Dry fly, size 10
Thread: Tan
Body: Coloured foam, cut to shape
Hackle & wings: Grizzle cock
Legs: Knotted pheasant strands

Whether you see the real insects about or not, a daddy can be an effective fly for the bigger-mouthed species. Last summer, a close friend caught a large grass carp on this fly. They are readily available commercially, and great fun to try.

Species: Chub, carp

WOODCOCK & HARE'S LUG

Hook: Traditional wet fly 10-20
Body: Sparsely dubbed hare's mask over orange thread
Hackle: 2-2½ turns of woodcock

No seeker of the smaller coarse fishes should be without a few small spider patterns in their box. Many of these brilliant traditionals work well and the soft hackle makes a spider easily sucked in by even a dainty mouth. Don't be afraid to go small for fish such as dace and roach, with sizes 16 or smaller especially useful.

Species: Dace, roach, rudd, chub, carp, bream, tench

DAIWL BACH

Hook: Nymph 10-16

Thread: Brown or black

Chin & tail: Red hackle fibres

Body: Peacock herl, natural or dyed

Rib: Copper wire or holographic tinsel

Cheeks (optional): Dyed biot or jungle cock

This general fit nymph has proven especially useful for roach and rudd fishing on small stillwaters such as canals and ponds. Again, take some smaller versions – a 16 is handy where fish reject a trout-sized artificial.

Species: roach, rudd, carp, bream

FRESHWATER SHRIMP

Hook: Buzzer or shrimp 10-16

Thread: Brown

Underbody: Turns of lead wire

Body/legs: Hare's Ear spectrablend dubbing/partridge fibres

Back: 'Nymph skin' or polythene strip

Rib: 5lb monofilament line

Various fish consume freshwater shrimps and a suitable copy is especially useful on running water. For a healthy current, well-weighted patterns can be created with turns of lead wire underneath the body dubbing.

Species: roach, dace, chub, barbel

PINK SHRIMP *Variant*　　CAENIS

Hook: Shrimp or grubber 12-16
Head: Small gold bead
Thread: Pink, fine
Tail: White game fibres
Body: Pink glister dubbing
Rib: 4lb mono
Shellback: Pink flash foil

Urban fishing specialist Theo Pike showed me this great little catcher on London's River Wandle, where it has accounted for numerous roach, chub and dace. Pink is not the most natural colour, but coarse fish seem to find it curiously attractive, especially where baits such as maggots are regularly introduced.

Species: roach, chub and dace

Hook: Fine wire 18-26
Thread: Ultra-fine white
Tail: Micro fibbets
Body: White biot
Wings: White antron
Thorax: Fine black dubbing

Sometimes fish such as dace or rudd will browse on miniscule flies such as caenis at the surface. It can be a recipe for utter frustration – unless of course you have some suitable artificials in your box! Present these on as fine a leader as you dare.

Species: Dace, rudd, roach

EGG FLIES

Hook: Wide gape size 10-12
Thread: To suit
Body: Bright yarn in yellow, red or other
Additional weight (optional): Lead wire underneath dressing

Egg flies were originally conceived to imitate the eggs of salmon and other fish. Typically though, modern egg flies are more useful to arouse interest from coarse fishes such as carp and tench, simulating feed such as corn and boilies. Natural they are not, but very useful.

Species: Tench, carp, chub, barbel

LIVING DAMSEL

Hook: Short shank nymph 8-12
Thread: Dark olive
Eyes: Lead nymph eyes
Tail: Knotted marabou
Thorax: Olive dubbing
Thorax cover: Pheasant
Rib: Gold tinsel
Legs: Olive dyed partridge

These readily-available nymphs have a terrific wiggle and are fun to use wherever the naturals are found. They have proved especially attractive to chub on weedy streams. Carp can also be persuaded to follow one, although getting them to take is often another matter!

Species: Chub, carp, bream

WOOLLY BUGGER

Hook: Long shank lure 2-10
Thread: Strong, to suit
Head (optional): Brass bead, sequin collar
Body: Palmered cock hackle over chenille
Rib: Oval tinsel or wire
Tail/legs: Marabou with a hint of krystal flash or similar

A really adaptable general lure which will tempt a whole range of species. White or flashy versions can work well for perch or jack pike, but more sombre colours are better for other fish. Olive or black are favourites. Weighted heads are useful for fast-flowing or deep water and a sequin produces resistance and an extra wiggle.

Species: chub, bream, perch, pike

For Roach & Rudd

MICRO CDC BUZZER

Perhaps the most useful of all the small nymphs I have used for stillwater rudd and roach, small suspending or painfully-slow sinking buzzers are highly effective. From observing both species, I believe that the fish are willing takers of a fly presented to hang just above them. Heavier, faster-sinking artificials seem to be regarded with a great deal more suspicion or ignored outright. Rudd especially, will happily point upwards to intercept a wet fly – but will seldom stoop for one. Recommended sizes are 14-20, although 16 is perhaps the optimum. Avoid heavy hooks; an emerger or light nymph hook is ideal. Body materials are a matter of personal choice – flexifloss, pheasant, stripped quill or simply layers of thread are all suitable. Select the finest rib you can find though. Common buzzer colours are black or olive – although red is a very handy substitute in water with extra colour.

A little tuft of CDC creates the suspending/slow sinking effect. White is my preferred colour, simply because it stands out well against weedy or dark backdrops.

Hook: 14-20 emerger
Thread: Ultra-fine black, olive or red
Breathers: Tuft of white CDC
Thorax: 3-4 turns of peacock herl
Body: Pheasant, stripped herl, biot or thread
Rib: Fine flat tinsel

Tying instruction *(see opposite)*

1. Catch some fine thread on the hook, leaving a little gap for the finish. You can also debarb the fly first.

2. Run the thread down the hook in tight turns, catching in your body materials (two strands of dyed black pheasant tail in this case).

3. Catch in some fine tinsel as you bring the thread back towards the head, stopping a little early to allow space for the thorax. You can stretch the tinsel a little first to get a finer diameter.

4. Wind the body material back towards the head evenly. Tie off with thread.

5. Now apply an even rib, tying off in the same place.

6. Bunch a few white CDC fibres between thumb and forefinger and tie these flat just behind the eye of the hook. You can also pass two or three turns of thread in front of the tuft to prevent the CDC covering the eye of the hook.

7. Trim off and cover the stub with turns of thread to leave room for the thorax area.

8. Catch in a single strand of peacock herl and make a thorax with 3-4 turns.

9. Whip finish fly. Add a tiny drop of varnish to the thread as you do so – this is preferable to applying it to the finished knot and spoiling the CDC.

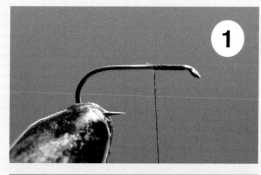

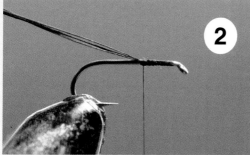

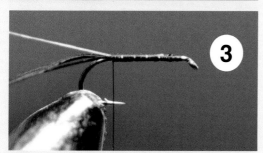

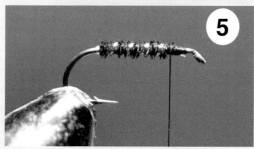

FISHING THE BUZZERS

Suspending buzzers can be fished singly, or in a team. An excellent set-up is to fish a dry fly on the point, plus one or two buzzers on droppers to hang just under the surface. Don't be too surprised if you catch more than one fish on the same cast!

211

Dark & Deadly!

BLACK & PEACOCK

Fly tyers can become obsessed with clever or complex patterns but some of the simplest of traditional flies still claim more than their share of fish. The Black and Peacock is just such a fly. And in fact where coarse fish are concerned, I can scarcely think of a pattern that has earned me more bites or caught more species of different fish, especially on still waters. Ok, so it's not rocket science to tie. It's a piece of cake, which is why I wanted to include it here. Even if you have sausages for fingers or have never tied a fly before, this is an easy fly to tie – but deadly nonetheless! It's especially good for roach and rudd, but I've also had carp, chub and even the odd skimmer bream and perch take this old favourite.

Hook: 8-18
Thread: Black
Body: Peacock herl
Head hackle: Black hen
Tag (optional): Mylar or any fluorescent material

So incredibly simple, but another brilliant pattern that no flyfisher should be without. It doesn't strictly resemble anything, but for some reason, snail-feeding fish seem to love this timeless killer. A size 12-16 is a fine catcher of roach and rudd, whilst for cruising carp a size 8 or 10 is hardly too big.
Species: Roach, rudd, bream, tench, chub, carp

Tying instruction *(see opposite)*

1. Take a hook and fasten thread with a few turns, catching in 2-3 peacock herl strands as you go down the shank.

2. Stop before you reach above the hook barb. Now wrap the herl around your tying thread – this will make the fly more durable.

3. Make a nice, even body with close turns of peacock. Stop and secure the herl when you get towards the eye, remembering to leave enough room for the hackle.

4. Tie in a black hen hackle – pick one in proportion to your hook size.

5. Wind on 3-5 turns of hen hackle, before stroking back. Whip finish, adding a little drop of varnish.

This rudd couldn't resist a Black & Peacock twitched slowly just under the surface.

Grub's Up!

THE MAGGOT FLY

Flies resembling 'bait' are sure to divide opinion amongst anglers, but some patterns are useful enough to merit inclusion. Such is the maggot fly. On many popular waters maggots are in such wide use that, contrary to the views of those hard-nosed purists, the fish find these grubs virtually natural.

Are we bordering on bait fishing? Admittedly, yes – but sometimes a fly rod is the perfect way to catch fish feeding on maggots. The simple act of dispensing with floats, swimfeeders and weights is in itself a huge advantage at times, for example in painfully shallow water or where the fish have grown wary of loud splashes or conspicuous terminal tackle.

I make no apologies therefore: grub patterns are very useful either alone, or even amongst some loose fed real maggots. Traditional, no; effective, yes. The grub will work for just about any coarse fish that can be tempted on maggots. Having tried various materials, the rim of a latex glove is the best I've found. Many of these are even powdered and this along with the 'give' of the material, provide a suitably soft feel.

Hook: Nymph 10-14
Thread: White
Body: Rim cut from white latex glove
Head: Peacock herl or coloured bead

1. Take a latex glove and locate the rim at the 'wrist'. By rolling back this ridge you can find the thickness you require, from fairly thick to very fine.

2. With a sharp craft knife or scissors, cut off a 4in section as close to the ridge as possible.

3. Make up a base of white thread along the hook shank in touching turns, passing down the shank and back to just before the eye.

4. Tie in the glove section as you return back with the thread. Gently stretching the latex as you go will produce a thinner, neater base.

5. Add 2-3 tight turns of thread above the hook barb to trap the latex in place. Then return the thread to just behind the eye.

6. Now wind the latex onto the hook steadily under a little tension to create an even body. Leaving enough room for the head, tie off the latex tightly with a few turns and trim carefully.

7. Add a little dubbing material of your choice to the tying thread.

8. Make two or three turns of dubbing, before a whip finish and a drop of varnish.

TIP
Water resistant markers such as pantone pens can be used to create different colours. Yellow or red are good variations here.

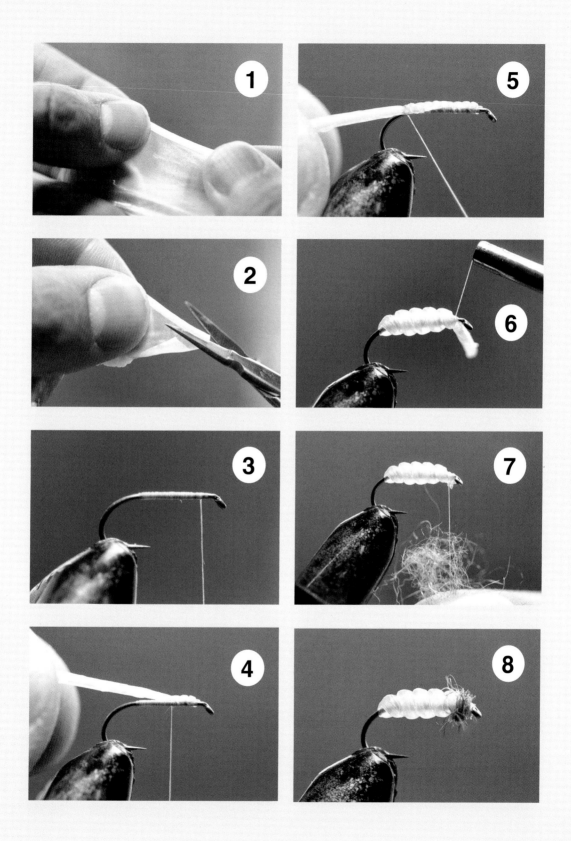

The Deep Destroyer!

THE JIG FLY

Deep water is a common challenge when fishing for predatory species. Fail to get the fly down to the fish and you won't catch them, it can be that simple. In cold conditions, species such as perch and zander, in particular, can be nailed to the deck and unwilling to grab something that sails way over their heads.

Besides sinking quickly, this style of fly also has the classic up and down 'jigging' action which predators love, allowing you to hop the fly slowly along the bottom if required. Towards the end of the retrieve you can also use the rod tip, much like a lure angler. In water from 10ft or greater depths, this is an exceptionally useful fly. The sample here is a typical perch size, but pike and zander will accept much larger versions.

Hook: Size 2-6 lure
Thread: Kevlar
Head: Dumbbell eyes, tied to underside of hook, Clouser-style.
Tail: Bright EP or synthetic fibres with a few strands of flash material
Body: Fritz or bright synthetic dubbing
Collar: Grizzle hackle

1. Take the hook and run a layer of thread over the first few millimetres, building a thread base to take the dumbbell eyes.

2. With tight wraps of thread, fasten the eyes above the hook (ie opposite side to the hook point). Pass the thread round from different angles, aiming for a snug, even covering.

3. Add a drop of varnish or a little epoxy to secure the head. You could even do several flies at a time, in a batch. When it's dry, flip the hook around in the vice so that it sits hook point down.

4. Now take your flexible tail materials (eg EP Fibres, Alien Hair, Krystal Flash etc) and combine carefully. I like a mix of solid colour, along with some flashy or tinselly strands. You want enough length to cover the hook shank, but also to give a trailing tail of similar length to the hook itself. The securest way to do this is to use roughly twice the required measurement of material (eg around 6in for a 3in fly), which will later be doubled back securely as we tie it in.

5. Measure the mixed strands between your fingers and grasp at the half way point. Now tie in just behind the head, securing with a few tight wraps.

6. Fold the rest of the materials back to double up the thickness of the tail, securing with wraps of thread all the way down the hook shank. Stop just before the hook point.

7. Take a good pinch of bright dubbing and add to the thread. You could also use fritz.

8. Wind the sparkly dubbing or fritz in even turns and secure just behind the eyes.

9. Now tie in a section of grizzle hackle.

10. Make four or so turns of hackle and secure with the thread, before whip finishing and adding a spot of varnish.

Pint-sized fly for pike

THE FROST BITE

There is a certain nonsense which always afflicts pike angling when it comes to lure and fly sizes. Someone always has to go bigger than the rest – indeed, some would have it that only the biggest artificials are capable of taking the big fish. It simply isn't true! Even big pike feed on smaller prey and furthermore, the bigger the flies become, the more they cast like wet socks! What I would never deny is the value of a big fly when searching a huge lake or in murky water. But for most other situations, a moderately-sized pike fly is perfectly adequate and a good deal more pleasant to cast. For new converts to pike on the fly, I would recommend an eight weight flyline, a modest pike fly – and a small water with plenty of pike!

The 'Frost Bite' resulted from experiments on small waters such as canals and drains. It casts effortlessly on an 8wt set-up and has a bit of everything: some light and some dark; some flash and a bright target point. The black deer hair ensures that it sinks very slowly which is ideal for those shallow, weedy, pike-infested waters where lures continually snag.

Hook: Sakuma phantom, size 1
Thread: Kevlar
Head: Epoxy & 3D eyes
Gills: Hot orange chickabou
Wing: Black bucktail or deer hair
Sides: Grizzle hackles
Body/tail: White EP fibres/ a few strands of flash material

Tying instruction *(see opposite)*

1. Catch the thread on the hook and run it about half way down the shank.

2. Blend together some EP fibres with a few strands of krystal flash or similar. Take 4in (10cm) of blended material and tie down firmly with tight turns of thread.

3. You can apply some varnish for extra strength between stages – this adds durability.

4. Select two matching grizzle cock hackles, clipping down to match body length.

5. Next tie in two grizzle hackles along the hook shank, one each side, using the pinch and loop technique. These should be measured to finish just short of the body fibres. Add more varnish.

6. Now for the gills: select two matching chickabou feathers.

7. Trim down the stalks to leave the fluffy ends and tie in the plumes one each side, binding down tightly.

8. Take a decent pinch of black buck tail and tie in as an over-wing.

9. Finally, the head is created by building up thread and then coating in epoxy.

Let this go tacky before adding two holographic eyes. You may also want to use pliers to crush the barb to a 'bump' for a more pike-friendly fly.

Predator Fly Tying Tips

Adding Strength: Flies for toothy fish require a tougher construction if they are not to fall to bits quickly. This can be done with several useful tricks.

★ Varnish can be applied at intervals throughout the tying. This helps prevent materials coming unstuck after encounters with teeth.

★ When using fritz, chenille or other body materials, strength can be added by wrapping around your tying thread *(see below)*.

Movement is Key

★ With streamers and lures of all sizes, a little extra resistance can produce extra wiggle. Special cones can be purchased, or little plastic lips cut from any suitable container and attached. Simpler still with smaller flies is to add a sequin to increase resistance *(see below)*.

★ Choice of materials also affects movement greatly. Too much bulk can result in less fluidity and a heavier fly. Rabbit strip is perhaps the ultimate in producing wiggle.

Snag Proofing

★ Weed guards are another useful extra device. 20-30lb mono is best, tied on just down the hook bend first. As the fly is finished, the other end can then be whipped close to the eye.

★ Other ways of creating a fly less prone to weeding include using bucktail or other stiff-ish material to afford the hook point some protection. Or try tying the fly with dumb-bell eyes, Clouser-style to fish upside down.

INDEX

USEFUL LINKS

DG Fishing

The author's own website offers flies, featured articles, photography and a lively blog with further fishing adventures.

www.dgfishing.co.uk

The Angling Trust

This is the organisation which unites all anglers into one powerful body, regardless of their preferred methods. From encouraging newcomers, to fighting pollution, abstraction and other threats, every one of us should be a member.

www.anglingtrust.net

Pike Anglers Club of Great Britain (PAC)

A great club, working hard to protect and promote pike and fishing.

www.pacgb.co.uk

Pike Fly-Fishing Association (PFFA)

www.pffa.co.uk

Cookshill Fly Tying

This is an excellent source of traditional and hard-to-find materials.

www.cookshill-flytying.co.uk

Deer Creek

They produce fantastic new ideas and innovative products for flytyers, such as many of the 3D eyes which I use on my pike patterns.

www.deercreek.co.uk

The Wye and Usk Foundation

This organisation does invaluable conservation work, and administers excellent fishing for coarse species, with especially good stretches to cast a fly for chub, pike and barbel.

www.wyeuskfoundation.org

British Float Tube Association

wwwbfta.co.uk

Barbel Society

Its website includes sound advice on safe catch-and-release practice.
www.barbelsociety.co.uk

Westcountry Angling Passport

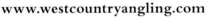

This is an excellent, conservation-minded scheme, offering plenty of wild, untapped fishing for coarse fish and for trout and salmon.
www.westcountryangling.com

Bob James

Bob offers guided fishing trips in some stunning locations. The ideal tutor for those who wish to catch chub, barbel and other species on the fly.
www.bobjamesfishing.net

Hardy Greys

They produce a wide selection of top quality fly tackle, from useful river fishing accessories to purpose-made pike rods, as used by the author himself.
www.hardyfishing.com
www.greysfishing.com

The Angling Times

A paper which is still the best source of features and news on all things coarse fishing, with regular contributions from the author!
www.gofishing.co.uk